The Lo-Tech Navigator

To
Captain Thomas H. Sumner of Boston
who, in 1837, solved the mystery

The Lo-Tech Navigator

Tony Crowley

SEAFARER BOOKS

SHERIDAN HOUSE

First published in the UK by:
Seafarer Books
102 Redwald Road
Rendlesham
Woodbridge
Suffolk IP12 2TE

And in the USA by:
Sheridan House Inc.
145 Palisade Street
Dobbs Ferry N.Y. 10522
www.sheridanhouse.com

UK   ISBN 0 95427 503 9
USA   ISBN 1 57409 191 3

British Library Cataloguing in Publication Data:
Crowley, Tony,
The lo-tech navigator
1.Navigation
I.Title
623.8 9

ISBN 0954275039

A CIP catalog record for this book is available from the
Library of Congress, Washington, DC

Text set digitally in 12/15pt Joanna

Typesetting and design by Louis Mackay
Illustrated by Tony Crowley

Printed in Great Britain at
The Lavenham Press Limited
Lavenham
Suffolk

Contents

Introduction

Today, with the rapid advances in science and technology, increasing numbers of sailors and boat owners venture across the world's oceans relying almost entirely on electronic aids and global positioning systems. In the unfortunate event of damage by an electric storm, equipment failure, disruption by a truculent government or space junk, they may be left struggling to master the mysteries of celestial navigation and, like the Flying Dutchman, doomed forever to circle the globe.

Many of the ideas which are presented in this book are intended for the benefit of those seafarers who wish to be less dependent on modern and expensive equipment and who want to discover how earlier navigators found their way safely across vast oceans. In the first part of the book, several gadgets are presented which focus on pilotage skills, the use of charts and the management of tidal and other information. The second half is devoted to the basics of navigating by the sun and the stars and how to make a selection of traditional instruments. Occasionally, the contents focus on unusual or novel solutions to navigational problems — so be prepared for the occasional whacky idea. For example, most navigators know that you can find your latitude in the northern hemisphere with the help of the Pole Star, but how do you find your longitude with the help of the same star? All is revealed in the chapter entitled 'The longitude game'. Practise the simple skills outlined in 'A handy sun compass', and amaze your shipmates or fellow survivors with your ability to locate the precise direction of east or west.

Each of the practical projects starts with a description of the device and, if appropriate, some historical background. This is followed by a list of materials and any special tools which may be required in its construction. Step-by-step instructions for making the device are provided along with notes on how to use it. All the ideas and projects presented have been thoroughly tested, but the reader is encouraged to consider ways in which they might be improved.

For most of the projects, only a few simple hand tools are required and the materials are easily obtainable. For example, the steering compass in the first chapter was made from a WC ball float, and Henry, the octant in the navigation section, was made mainly from junk and cost £2 ($3), yet produces results as good as those from a budget sextant. By all means support your local DIY store, but remember that in our throw-away world there is little need to purchase expensive or sophisticated fittings. Waste disposal sites and charity shops are stacked high with a wealth of reusable items and materials.

Finally, scattered among the projects is a collection of seafaring tales, puzzles, poetry and nautical oddities. It is hoped that these will be an additional source of entertainment as you browse through these pages in search of your next project.

Three compasses for the price of one

An emergency compass

Here is an easy start to the projects in this book. It is a simple compass which requires nothing more than the lid of a tin can and a fridge magnet.

The next time you open a tin can, save the lid, mark a line across it and float it in water. There's a good chance that the lid has some residual magnetism and that the line will return persistently to point in one direction. All you need do is find the lid's north–south axis, mark it permanently, and you have an emergency compass.

The lid's magnetic field can be given a boost by stroking its north–south axis with a permanent magnet. File off any sharp edges and smear a thin layer of vaseline on the upper side of the lid to prevent it from sliding underwater and sinking. Store it away carefully – you never know when you may need it.

A steering compass

My first boat was rather parish-rigged and although it had a good handbearing compass, the steering compass was made out of a plastic ball float from a WC cistern.

Cut open at the bottom, it held a pair of permanent rod magnets, and floated partially submerged in a bucket of sea water which served as a windshield and a reservoir. For gimbals, the bucket could be slung from the tiller. A de luxe version included a second container within the bucket which was slightly larger than the ball float. This arrangement permitted the compass to rotate freely and was very effective. Nowadays, my ball float compass lies abandoned at the bottom of a locker. I've toyed with the idea of restoring it to its original purpose but wonder what a plumber would make of those compass points.

A traditional dry card compass

The next compass is rather more efficient and much better looking. It's based on a traditional dry card compass, some of which were still to be found in merchant ships in the 1950s. Dry card compasses had a tendency to swing around, and an early, though incorrect, solution

was to blunt the pivot needle. In the 19th century, Lord Kelvin introduced a more effective damping method by designing a very light card with most of its weight concentrated on the perimeter. It had a jewel at its pivot and specially arranged magnetised needles suspended by silk thread, The compass here is based on Kelvin's ideas and the card weighs less than half an ounce (13g). There's no jewel at the centre, however, just a small brass disc with an indentation which pivots freely on a sharp needle. At sea, although the card rocks gently, it has good directional stability.

The compass shown here was made from the following materials:

- One sharp darning needle approximately 7cm in length
- Six needles ranging from 4cm to 6cm in length
- One light wooden hoop (e.g. embroidery hoop) about 18–20 cm in diameter
- Some transparent adhesive film
- A copy of a compass rose
- The centre piece of an old 45rpm record
- A walking stick tip or non-ferrous thimble

- A metal disc (non-ferrous) about 2mm thick and 10mm diameter (this could be cut from the shank of a tap)

- A wooden box with non-ferrous fittings

- A fridge magnet, or other permanent magnet

- An epoxy-based adhesive

1. With the head of a 2mm drill, make a small cone-shaped indentation in the centre of the metal disc. Glue the disc inside the thimble.

2. Enlarge the hole in the record centre and glue the thimble over it. This is the pivot cap.

3. Take the inner circle of the embroidery hoop. To reduce weight, slice it into two hoops and discard one piece.

4. Cut a piece of adhesive film so that it overlaps the hoop by about 1.5cm. Make a series of small cuts around the circumference of the film. Stretching the film as tight as possible, fold the outer edge over the hoop and back on itself.

5. Make a 'union jack' of small cuts across the centre of the adhesive film and push up the pivot cap through and against the adhesive side of the film.

6. Fit the outer section of the compass rose inside the hoop and press it face upwards against the adhesive underside of the film.

7. Lightly stroke a fridge magnet about a dozen times along the length of, and just above, each of the six needles. Lift the magnet sharply away at the end of each stroke. Check the needles' polarity by floating them in water on a small piece of cork.

8. Attach the needles to the adhesive side of the film so that their north-seeking poles align with the compass rose. Place them about 1cm apart and arrange the ends on the circumference of an imaginary circle around the centre piece (see photo). Place a backing strip of adhesive film over the needles to secure them in position.

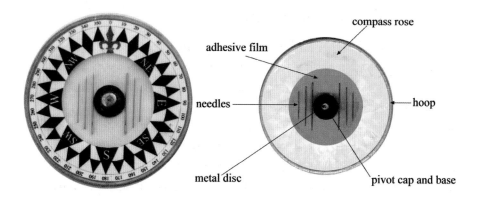

compass rose

adhesive film

needles

hoop

metal disc

pivot cap and base

9. Fix the long sharp pivot needle in a small block on the base of the wooden box. Although this needle may be ferrous, it won't affect the card. Check to see how well the card balances on the pivot and, if necessary, add some weight or adjust the needles slightly.

10. Place the north-seeking end of the card facing south and release it gently. It should return very gradually back to north in about two oscillations occupying a total of about 45 seconds.

If the needles ever need a boost, lift out the card and stroke them with a magnet through the adhesive film. Note that the sharp pivot needle is a potential hazard so place a piece of cork on the point and close the lid whenever the card is removed.

To make a compass box

From a length of plywood or MDF, cut four identical pieces with a 45° bevel as shown in the photograph. The lower section forms the sides of the box and the upper section, with a slot for a sheet of acetate, provides the lid. Join the pieces together with a strong adhesive and add a wooden base. Any nails, screws or hinges must be non-ferrous. A similar box with a solid lid may be used to store other objects such as a plastic sextant.

Compass variation and deviation

Owing to irregularities in the earth's magnetic structure, a compass rarely points to true north. The discrepancy is known as variation and is named east or west according to the direction in which the compass is deflected. Before the development of the chronometer some early navigators were able to use local variation as a crude guide to their longitude when crossing the Atlantic. At any particular place, however, variation isn't constant but gradually changes with time. Information on local variation is usually printed in the compass rose on a chart.

Local magnetic fields within a ship can cause the compass to lie in a different direction from the earth's magnetic field. This is known as deviation and is also named east or west according to the direction in which the compass is deflected from magnetic north. It can vary depending on the direction in which the vessel is heading and is caused by a variety of sources such as the ship's steel structure, electric cables, machinery or rigging. It can also be caused by metal objects left inadvertently near the compass – e.g. a radio, a knife or beer cans.

Note that deviation or variation west deflects the north-seeking end of a compass card to the left so the reading will appear higher than it is actually is.

With a variation or deviation east, the north end of the card is deflected to the right so the reading is lower.

During trials with the dry card compass, I was puzzled to discover a deflection of 15° west (i.e. the compass heading was 15° in excess of the true heading). Five of these degrees were due to variation but the remainder appear to have been caused by static electricity – the result of over-zealous polishing of the compass box.

On a small yacht, the deviation of the steering compass may be checked quite effectively by comparing different headings with those obtained from a handbearing compass held well clear of any interference. Any discrepancies can be noted on a deviation card placed near the compass.

A sailing personality quiz

Grade these items according to how well they describe you by circling one of the numbers:

2 = That's me!   1 = A bit like me   0 = Not me at all

I enjoy a quiet sail alone	2	1	0
I love to be photographed at the helm	2	1	0
I'm good at explaining things to others	2	1	0
I always get along with my shipmates	2	1	0

I usually avoid a crowded bar	2	1	0
I would wear a silly hat for a laugh	2	1	0
My advice on nautical matters is often sought	2	1	0
I hate missing a club social or outing	2	1	0

I prefer yachting books to yachties	2	1	0
I'd volunteer to climb to the top of the mast	2	1	0
I usually take charge in an emergency	2	1	0
I enjoy teamwork and group tasks	2	1	0

I don't mind being left alone aboard	2	1	0
I have a fund of sailing anecdotes and jokes	2	1	0
If others are wrong, I soon tell them	2	1	0
I enjoy singalongs and shanties	2	1	0

I prefer to make my own decisions	2	1	0
I'd volunteer to be the 'man overboard'	2	1	0
I give clear orders and instructions	2	1	0
I like visiting other boats and their crews	2	1	0

If lost at sea...

I would quietly study *Navigation for Dummies*	2	1	0
I would shout and wave at passing boats	2	1	0
I would reprimand the navigator	2	1	0
I would pool ideas with my shipmates	2	1	0

My birthday wish list would include …

a carton of foam earplugs	2	1	0
a loud and vulgar spinnaker	2	1	0
a solar-powered megaphone	2	1	0
a tug-of-war rope	2	1	0

....

Scoring

There are seven blocks with four items in each block. Add together
the scores for the first item in each block, then the scores for the
second item, and so on. The four totals relate directly to the four
sailing types described below and your highest score may indicate
the personality type which best describes you.

1. Loner. Self-contained and thoughtful. Definitely a singlehanded
cruising man or woman. Tolerates racing but will fail to round the
second buoy and will disappear over the horizon. Avoids sailing at
weekends and is usually found nursing a bottle of gin in a remote
creek. Fond of saying 'If you want something doing, best do it yourself.'

2. Attention-seeker. Though seldom a boat owner, is always a boon
to the club's entertainment committee. Will only race if there is a good
chance of winning or capsizing. Can be a little tiresome on a long-
distance cruise, and, if a non-swimmer, must always be tethered by a
harness. Fond of saying 'This sailing business is a bit of a laugh, eh?'

3. Leader. Admires Nelson, Hornblower, Queeg and Bligh. Usually
heard shouting angrily at partner when entering or leaving locks and
moorings. May be spotted pointing derisively from the committee
boat or the bar. Harbours a secret desire to fly the blue ensign. Fond
of saying 'A ship can only have one captain.'

4. Mixer. A good sort invariably found ordering and paying for drinks,
catching mooring lines, pushing open lock gates, fixing blocked heads
etc. A sociable cruising companion who genuinely prefers the 'hot bunk'
system. Fond of saying 'Come on you guys, let's all pull together.'

Gone with the wind

A handheld anemometer

This simple gadget measures the speed of the wind. It is based on the old pressure-plate anemometers that were occasionally used in aircraft or at high altitudes. The pressure plate is made from a strip of 1mm acetate held securely at the top of the device. It bends backwards along a graded scale according to the strength of the wind and springs back to zero when the wind drops. Unlike a pressure plate that is free to swing, it is less sensitive to light winds but works well from about a force 3 upwards. Like all anemometers, it invariably shows that the wind is not quite as strong as you imagine it to be.

Materials required

- A piece of plywood or MDF 180mm × 120mm × 4mm

- A short piece of broomhandle or dowelling as a handle

- A small sheet of 1mm clear acetate available from a hobbies shop

- Glue and woodstain etc

Instructions for assembly

Cut out a triangular shape with a short extension as shown in the photograph. Cut a slot in the dowelling and glue the two together. Use spare wood to make a small triangular support with a slot and attach it to the base. Cut a strip of acetate measuring 130mm × 8mm and glue it into the slot so that it extends about 120mm and can move freely. Sand all wooden edges to reduce turbulence.

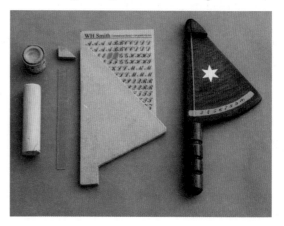

When marking out the scale, use the following angles as a guide. They are measured from where the acetate strip emerges from its support.

Force	0	3	4	5	6	7	8	9
Angle	0°	5°	10°	14°	18°	22°	26°	29°

To use the device, hold it steady in the direction of the wind and clear of any obstructions. The accuracy of the scale may be checked with the help of a manufactured handheld anemometer. If the wind is light, compare how the two react to the various settings of a hairdryer, or, with the help of an assistant, you could take it for a test drive in a car.

A de luxe version

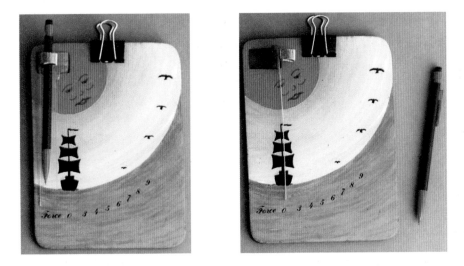

This nautical clipboard with its own wind gauge is based on the system outlined above. The pencil holder and acetate strip are attached to a small door in the clipboard. This is hinged by a pin running down through the clipboard and swings out to reveal the acetate strip ready for action.

I once discovered that the wind could play an old harmonica through a funnel at around force 4. I didn't persist with this experiment for therein lies madness.

Converting the Beaufort scale to knots

Admiral Beaufort's scale for wind and weather is known and used throughout the world, but it is not easy to remember. Here is a handy way of converting the wind force numbers to knots and vice versa.

- To convert the wind scale to knots, deduct 1 and multiply the remainder by 5.

  e.g. to convert from force 4: $4 - 1 = 3$. $3 \times 5 = 15$ knots.

- To convert knots to wind scale, divide the knots by 5 and add 1.

  e.g. to convert from 25 knots: $25/5 = 5$. $5 + 1 =$ force 6.

This method produces an average figure and is accurate up to force 8. It is particularly suitable for converting TV weather maps, which often display wind strength in multiples of five knots.

Test your knowledge of the wind

1. Wind blows from a high pressure to a low pressure area.
    ❏ True   ❏ False

2. Wind speed increases with height above sea level.
    ❏ True   ❏ False

3. A land-to-sea wind is steadier than a sea-to-land wind.
    ❏ True   ❏ False

4. Face the wind and the area of low pressure is towards your right.
    ❏ True   ❏ False

5. Wind coming from high ground is more turbulent than a surface wind.
    ❏ True   ❏ False

6. Around a prominent headland, the wind's speed lessens.
    ❏ True   ❏ False

7. The closer the isobars on a weather map, the faster the speed of the wind.
    ❏ True   ❏ False

8. In the Beaufort scale, a light breeze is stronger than a gentle breeze.
    ❏ True   ❏ False

9. A wind speed of 30 knots is a force 8 gale.
    ❏ True   ❏ False

10. Wind changing in a clockwise direction is said to veer.
    ❏ True   ❏ False

Check your answers on page 145.

A tide table holder

Mounted on a convenient bulkhead, this three-in-one storage device keeps your your tide tables to hand and can also be used to display the times and the state of the tide. An ideal solution for those who have a habit of mislaying tide tables or, having consulted them, forget the information. It happens to all of us eventually. You can use it to store pencils too.

The wheel can be used to show the time of the next high water and subsequent low water or the times of low water to high water.

Not only does the time wheel rotate, but it slides horizontally so it can be adjusted to display a duration from about five to seven hours. Having set the wheel, read the hour scale in conjunction with the three horizontal lines representing high, middle and low water. This will provide a rough check on the state of the tide. The device is suitable for those areas where tides rise and fall in a regular pattern, i.e. with the greatest movement occurring around mid tide. The version shown here was made in plywood but you could use MDF or similar.

Materials

- Front and back faces, wheel: 340mm × 110mm × 4mm

- Inner frame: 330mm × 15mm × 10mm

- A nut, bolt and washers

- A circular piece of felt

- Instant lettering, gold paint

- Varnish or woodstain, Araldite adhesive

Construction

Here are the main dimensions and method of assembly. Don't forget to include a short (2cm) horizontal slot in the front face behind the time wheel. To reach the end of the bolt when attaching the nut, you may need to cut a hole at the back. When the felt-backed wheel is sufficiently tight, cut away any spare bolt and secure the nut with some glue.

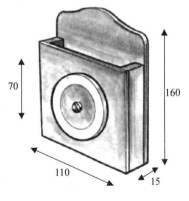

The twelfths rule

The three horizontal lines are a rough guide to the height of the tide. Another useful trick is the 'twelfths rule', which is applicable where tides are regular and have a duration of around six hours from high water to low water.

In the first hour after LW, the tide rises	1/12 of its range
In the second hour, it increases by	2/12 of its range
In the third hour, it increases by	3/12 of its range
In the fourth hour, it increases by	3/12 of its range
In the fifth hour, it increases by	2/12 of its range
In the sixth hour, it increases by	1/12 of its range

The same rule of thumb can be applied when estimating the fall in the tide from high to low water.

McGrath's revenge

A South Seas melodrama

The war in the Pacific was hardly over when the drums began beating. A continuous low-pitched rhythm throbbed from the cloud-capped hills overlooking the island of Nasuma. It rolled across the valleys, through the vanilla plantations, over the mangrove swamps and down to the harbour where the inter-island ferry *Ocean Flower* lay at her berth. Her decks were dusty and deserted. Not a soul or thing stirred aboard save for a small masthead flag which fluttered feebly at each passing breath of air. A lone figure walked slowly along the quayside, pausing occasionally to wipe his brow and rest before continuing on his way.

At the foot of the gangway, he stopped to inspect the vessel and noticed someone crouching by one of the lifeboats. 'What are you doing, Mr McGrath?' he shouted in a tone which carried some authority.

Kevin McGrath, First Mate of the *Ocean Flower*, arose from the boat deck holding a spanner in one hand and shading his eyes from the blinding glare of the sun with the other. 'I'm just checking the rails, sir,' he cried as he recognised the ship's master on the quayside below. 'Apparently, there's a loose one up here somewhere.'

'Belay that,' growled the Captain. 'I'd like a word in your ear.'

The Captain mounted the gangway slowly and reached the deck just as the mate stepped out into the alleyway. 'Is everything alright, sir?' asked Kevin and then added. 'If you don't mind me saying, you look worn out.'

'I'm fine,' replied the Captain abruptly. 'But what about our passengers?' He indicated with a thumb in the direction of the saloon further down the alleyway.

'Well, they're not overjoyed with the delay. Grimble, the Colonial Office fellow, says there'll be trouble if we don't sail by tomorrow. His wife is expecting another child and she was unwell last night. Then the war hero with the double-barrel name came hammering on my door so I escaped to the boat deck for a bit of peace. Apart from that everything is, as you might say, tickety-boo.'

The Captain shot Kevin an odd sort of look and continued, 'I'll speak to them later. We'll sail when I say and not a minute before.

I have some private business to clear up. If they pester you, tell them there's a hurricane warning or whatever. I'm sure you'll think of something.'

'Very good sir. I hope they'll swallow it.' Kevin turned and strolled away. 'The old devil's away with the fairies again,' he thought as he flicked yet another butt end with pinpoint accuracy into a bucket standing outside the galley.

The Captain stood alone on the deck, his eyes staring coldly at the distant horizon. Above him, the seagulls circled with their plaintive cries. From the saloon came the rattle of cutlery and the clinking of glasses; a canvas awning flapped in the breeze, and, somewhere on the ship's side, a discharge pipe opened and spewed forth its contents into the waters below. Whistling cheerfully, the ship's cook emerged from the galley and removed some freshly-risen dough from a nearby bucket, but of these sounds the Captain was unaware. Yet he was listening: listening intently to a sound which came from the hills, the sound of drums.

Miss Clarissa Twist, a college librarian, sat tight-lipped in the saloon of the *Ocean Flower* studying the menu. 'Green pea soup but no sippets, thank you,' she hissed to the little Chinese steward who bobbed his head and scuttled away. 'As I was saying, Mr McGrath, do you know a good cure for seasickness?'

Kevin stared at her thoughtfully and then replied, 'Oh I do, Miss Twist, indeed I do. The only real cure is to find a nice green tree and go and sit underneath it.'

Miss Twist smiled. 'How very droll. And can you tell us anything about that drumming in the hills?'

'Sure,' said Kevin. 'I've worked in these islands since before the war and those drums you hear are part of a ceremony held every ten years in honour of Owata-Pekka.'

'Really?' replied Miss Twist. 'Is he an important chief?'

'No, I think yer man's a fertility god. But don't be alarmed, the mountain people are harmless and you'll sleep safely tonight.'

Miss Twist blushed and made a mental note to remove the parasol from under her pillow.

A silence fell over the saloon, broken at intervals when Grimble junior slurped his soup, and several minutes passed before anyone else spoke. Resplendent in a green velour smoking jacket, Major Spencer Canning-Horsham (Catering Corps – retired) carefully wiped his moustache with the edge of his napkin and waited for the attention of the other diners. 'Look, I don't know how you good people feel about being delayed here, but personally I find it damn annoying. I mean to say, I'll miss the golf club dinner and dance if we don't sail tonight.' 'And,' he thought to himself, 'that bounder Carruthers will be hanging around Gloria Ponsonby, the new nurse. So young, so fragile and so vulnerable. What a divine creature! I haven't seen such shapely ankles in many a long day.'

The others at the table were nodding in agreement and for a worrying moment he wondered if they could read his thoughts, then Grimble, the man from the Colonial Office, spoke.

'I've tried to speak to the Captain but he's not been answering his door and my wife is getting quite anxious. Has he given you any reason for our delay, Mr McGrath?'

Kevin mentioned the hurricane warning and added that the Captain didn't want to take unnecessary risks.

'A hurricane warning?' echoed Miss Twist. 'But I listened to the wireless all morning. The weather forecast followed the church service from Samoa – the vicar there is such a charming man. I know his wife very well, we serve on the ladies social committee at Government House. She's one of the Woode-Smythes from Bagshot, you know. Now where was I? Oh yes, I heard the weather forecast for the islands and there were certainly no hurricane warnings.'

Kevin groaned inwardly as all eyes turned in his direction. He took a deep breath and prepared plan (b): an unusually low tide and the risk of *Ocean Flower* running aground on the reef.

The brass clock on the bulkhead chimed twice and as the Captain heaved himself to his feet, his hand slipped on the edge of the desk at which he had been dozing and sent a half-empty whisky bottle crashing to the deck. The clear liquid formed a pool around the broken glass and started to drain away in a stream towards the doorway. The telephone rang several times but he ignored it. He lurched drunkenly across the cabin and struggled to open the porthole. Fresh air flowed into the cabin and he gulped at it eagerly. In a nearby cabin, someone was whining a tuneless refrain, but before he could close the porthole, the drumming started again. What did it all mean? He could put up with the voices that came at night but not the drums; they were driving him insane. Ashore, he had found some escape from the relentless pounding. It had been so peaceful there. He remembered the daylight streaming through stained-glass windows, the overpowering fragrance of incense and flowers, and the rows of candles flickering beneath the statues. Once more he heard his footsteps echoing on the stone floor as he walked towards the church door. And then the drums returned. With each step, they became louder and louder. If only he could stay there, they might leave him alone.

But it was no use: he had to leave and face the demons that were taunting him. There was no point in telling the passengers, though, they would only laugh. Such idle and arrogant people – but they kept the *Ocean Flower* in business. 'I don't know how McGrath can stand them, but then perhaps he's on their side. I never did like the fellow. Doesn't show enough respect for my liking. He's probably after my job if the truth is known. I'll have to get rid of him somehow and the sooner the better.' He staggered out of his cabin and stumbled across the wooden deck. For several moments he leaned against the rails ranting incoherently to himself, his bloodshot eyes staring wildly at the distant hills, and his bulky figure silhouetted against the burning blue of the Pacific sky.

In her small cabin on the boat deck, Miss Clarissa Twist was busy at her needlepoint whilst happily humming her favourite hymn. Midway through a crescendo in 'And was Jerusalem builded here' she heard a sudden noise and a cry outside the porthole. She put down her work and and peered out anxiously. 'Coooeee… is anyone there?'

But there was only silence and no sign of a disturbance.

'Well, that did give me a turn,' she whispered nervously as she resumed her task, a present for her favourite niece, Hermione, currently serving a five-year sentence at boarding school in England's green and pleasant land.

The tiffin gong sounded aboard the *Ocean Flower* and the passengers assembled in the saloon for tea. Several eagerly tucked into a large plate of cucumber sandwiches made from freshly baked bread.

McGrath noted the Captain's empty chair and wondered what could possibly interest the old man ashore. 'Were he a bit younger, I'd understand, but he's sixty if he's a day. Ah, it's a queer old world, sure enough.' His thoughts were rudely interrupted by the major's braying voice.

'McGrath, inform the Captain that we wish to speak to him as soon as possible. We've been delayed long enough. The man is always

AWOL. Frankly, it's a bad show, a damn bad show! And no more of your hurricane warnings and all that blarney about the tides!'

Kevin nodded. How he would love to sort out this pompous idiot. Then, all of a sudden, the small Chinese steward came rushing in babbling hysterically.

'Mr Mate, sir, you come plenty damn quick! Sailors catch big big fish... him on deck now. One bloody mess! Hurry please!'

Kevin leapt to his feet and followed the steward out of the saloon. Immediately all the passengers started talking and Miss Twist paled as she struggled to find a bottle of smelling salts in her handbag. The major arose. 'I suggest that the ladies remain here while a couple of us chaps go and see if we can be of any assistance. This kind of thing often happens. The natives land sharks without taking any precautions. It sounds like a twenty-foot rokea: a frightful butcher. Flashes like a hurled lance through the water. Bite you in half as soon as look at you.'

Miss Twist gave a feeble cry and fainted.

'Yes,' he continued, stepping over her prostrate figure. 'Seen it happen once. Ghastly sight. Couldn't eat fish for months. Wonder where the first aid kit is?'

'Thank you, Major, but there is no need for any medical assistance.' Ashen-faced, Kevin stood in the saloon doorway.

'But what about the men who caught the shark?' asked the major, looking puzzled. 'We understood there was an accident.'

Kevin shook his head slowly. 'No, they're alright. They were just cutting it open and there's some clearing up to be done – a few loose ends.' He paused and turned to the major. 'Do you still wish to see the Captain?'

'Indeed I do, sir, and I intend to give him a piece of my mind – and there's no lie!'

Kevin gestured towards the open door. 'Well, I think you'll find that he's just come out on deck.'

A tide abacus

This bulkhead or portable indicator was designed to provide a simple and rapid method of finding the height of the tide at any time between high and low water. It's particularly suitable in areas where tides occur twice daily, such as the coasts of western Europe. In keeping with other tide calculation methods, the duration and range must first be obtained from tables issued for a standard port and adjusted, if necessary, for a secondary port. As with other methods, the device isn't infallible.

The tables are arranged according to a formula which assumes that tides rise or fall with the greatest movement occurring around the mid tide; the same sine-wave formula that's used to describe the movement of a pendulum. There are, however, certain areas of coastline – e.g. the Solent – where tides follow an irregular pattern. In addition, various meteorological effects, such as atmospheric pressure, strong offshore or onshore winds, and heavy rainfall, can interfere with the accuracy of tidal predictions. Within these limitations, and used in those situations where an approximation is acceptable, the device will provide results that are usually more accurate than those obtained through some graphical solutions or the 'twelfths rule'.

Materials required

- Two tables as reproduced in Appendix 1

- Two pieces of broomstick or dowelling for rollers, each 120mm × 22mm

- Four short pieces of dowelling as axles for the rollers, each 20mm × 3mm

- One piece of plywood or MDF 260mm × 80mm × 10mm
- Adhesive, woodstain, varnish, instant lettering
- Transparent adhesive film

Assembling the abacus

1. Into the ends of each length of broomstick, drill a 3mm hole to accommodate a short piece of dowelling. Photocopy the two tables to the required size. Cover the tables with a layer of transparent adhesive film and glue them to the rollers.

2. Cut out the wood frame and roller supports as shown below. Drill 3mm holes right through the supports to accommodate the short lengths of dowelling. Attach the supports to the frame leaving sufficient space for the rollers.

3. Give the frame a coat of woodstain. When this is dry, smudge a small area at the top and bottom of the frame with yellow paint as a background for instant lettering. Complete the frame with a coat of clear varnish.

4. Place some wood glue into the holes at the ends of each roller, and place these into position on the frame. Tap the short lengths of dowelling through the supports and into the rollers. The tide abacus is now ready for duty.

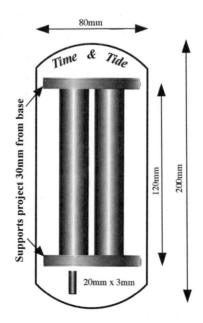

Using the abacus

When using the abacus, note that the time is always given from low water. This will be from the last low water if the tide is rising, and from the next low water if the tide is falling. Having consulted tide tables to determine the duration and the range of the tide, turn the rollers until the appropriate scales are next to each other.

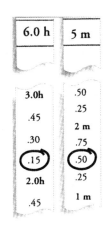

For example, suppose the tide has a duration of 6 hours and a range of 5 metres, the tables show that at 2 hours and 15 minutes from low water the tide will have reached 1.5 metres above low water.

If the duration and/or the range of the tide are between the values of the printed scales, turn the rollers so that the scales on either side of the required value may be seen.

For example, in a duration of 5.25 hours and a range of 6 metres, the height 3 hours after low water is approximately 3.8 metres. If the duration or the range of the tide lies beyond the largest scale, find a scale which represents half the desired figure and double the results. Or, if the desired figure lies below the smallest scale, find a scale which is double the required figure and halve the data.

Perhaps making the abacus sounds too much of a hassle. Why not paste the tables on two short lengths of broomstick and use them without a supporting frame? Alternatively, photocopy the tables on sheets of clear acetate and place one sheet over the other so that the required scales coincide. Or, paste the two tables on a card and use a straight edge across the tables to obtain the necessary data.

A fatal flaw

Here is a nautical version of an old riddle. Some people see the solution almost immediately, whereas others puzzle over it for hours – even days.

One cold and wet evening, an old cargo ship was lurching slowly across the North Atlantic. The third mate was brewing some coffee in the chartroom and the lookout huddled miserably behind the bridge dodger to avoid the rain. In the radio shack, the ship's radio officer was listening to some music from a French station. He sat nodding sleepily by the receiver and his head sank lower and lower until it was almost resting on the bench in front of him and he fell asleep. In his dream, he imagined he was living in Paris at the time of the Revolution and was on his way to the guillotine jeered by a large and violent crowd. Struggling desperately for his life, he was dragged up the steps to the platform and his neck laid across the fatal plank. Stricken with absolute terror he awaited the falling blade. At that very moment, the third mate popped his head around the radio room door. Seeing the operator asleep, he leaned across and tapped him smartly on the back of his neck with a teaspoon. 'Wake up, Sparks, coffee's ready,' he called. To his horror, the radio operator fell dead at his post!

The problem

Although such a fatality is possible, what evidence does the story contain which proves that it cannot have happened?

Answer on page 145.

A handy sun compass

Shipwrecked without a compass? Your shipmates will gaze in awe as you salute the sun with an outstretched hand and mysteriously divine the exact direction of east or west.

The sun rises in the east and sets in the west — give or take up to 30°, but there may come a time when you'll need to know the exact direction but haven't got a compass. Here is a neat trick which will help find the direction of east within an hour or two after sunrise, or west within an hour or two before sunset. To use it, you'll need to know roughly how many degrees the sun is north or south of the equator (i.e. its declination), have some idea of your latitude, and be able to measure angles with your hands.

To find the sun's declination

At the equinoxes (21 March and 23 September) the sun is over the equator

After one month it is	12° from the equator
After two months it is	20° from the equator
After three months (21 June and 21 December) it is	almost 24° from the equator
After four months it is	20° from the equator
After five months it is	12° from the equator
After six months it is	back over the equator

So find a way to remember 12, 20 and 24 (e.g. 12 + 8 + 4 = letters LHD = left hand drive: that sort of thing) and then you are ready to work out the declination. For example, suppose the sun is observed on 6 May. On 21 March the sun was over the equator. By 21 April it was about 12° north. By 21 May it will be about 20° north. As a rough estimate, on 6 May it is about 16° north.

Measuring angles with your hands

The next stage is to have a way of measuring angles with your hand. Viewed at arm's length, one finger covers an angle of about 2°. A two-finger gesture spans about 8°. A closed fist subtends an angle of about 10°; extend the thumb and the angle increases to 15°. A wide open hand can encompass an angle of 20° or more. By combining hands and fingers, a variety of angles may be obtained. These are average figures but you can check your own measurements with the help of a sextant or compass – especially if you have large hands or your knuckles graze the pavement.

To find the direction of east

Suppose the sun is 16° north of the equator and your latitude is 35° north. Four outstretched fingers at arm's length should encompass an angle of about 16°. Align them with the horizon with the finger nearest north touching the sun. Rotate the span of the fingers down by an amount equal to your latitude (e.g. 35°). Then slide the span at right angles to this line until the finger nearest south touches the horizon. You have now located the direction of east.

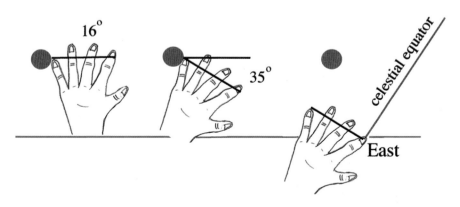

What happens is that when you rotate your fingers according to your latitude, the finger furthest from the sun aligns with the celestial equator. Then, when you slide the fingers down at right angles, it follows the path of the celestial equator to the horizon, a point which is due east (or west). Look back at this example and puzzle out what you would do if you were on or near the equator.

What if the declination is south?

If the sun is 16° south, the procedure from 35° north is almost identical, but now the sun is south of the celestial equator. Place the finger nearest south on the sun and rotate the span of the four fingers upwards by an amount equal to your latitude. Once again, slide your hand at right angles to this line until the finger nearest north touches the horizon. This is the direction of east.

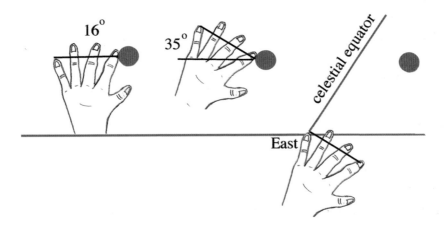

When the sun is low on the horizon, you may have to slide your hand up to the horizon to locate east or west. Finding west at sunset is the mirror image of the procedures outlined above, but if you can visualise the general direction of the celestial equator (according to your latitude), you will have little difficulty in rotating your hand in the correct direction. The procedure works almost anywhere except in higher latitudes during midsummer when it tends to place east or west a few degrees towards the nearest pole. Practise the method afloat or ashore and compare your findings with a compass reading.

The time of sunset

The finger at the other end of the span indicates where the sun will rise or set on the horizon. By measuring back to the sun from the setting position and dividing by 15° per hour, you should get an idea of when sunset will occur.

An oddity

There is another way of locating east or west from the sun, but it is more of a curiosity than anything else. In summer, when the sun is exactly east, it is rising in a latitude 90° away. For example, in the summer months when the sun crosses east in latitude 51° N it is rising in 39° S. The same is true of west at sunset. So, armed with sunrise and sunset timetables for different latitudes and a watch, you can determine the direction of east (or west). On the other hand, it would be interesting to discover why you took to the liferaft with these tables but no compass.

Rope trick

Which is the right and wrong way?

1

a   b

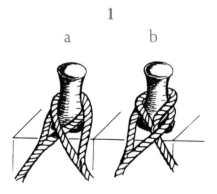

2

a   b

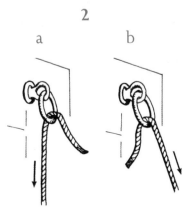

3

a

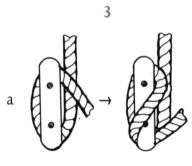

b

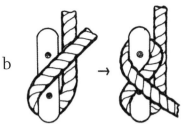

4

a

b

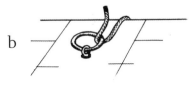

Answers on page 145.

A drogue log

The history of measuring speed at sea is awash with all kinds of ingenious devices. Among the earlier solutions was the chip log, which consisted of a wooden quadrant attached to a reel of marked line. With the log hove and floating astern, speed was measured by the

amount of line that ran out in a specified time. Other methods included the level of water forced up an L-shaped glass tube, towed rotators linked to registering dials and retractable impellers. Many contemporary logs rely on electro-magnetic pulses, and the latest employ satellite signals. Less well known are the drogue or drag logs which were used during the latter half of the 18th century and were the invention of Pierre Bouguer, a distinguished French scientist.

Bouguer's log consisted of a metal globe towed astern by a line that was attached to a lever mounted inboard. The pull of the line was resisted by a spring attached to the lever. The faster the ship moved through the water, the greater the movement of the lever over a scale graduated for speed. Although there were several variations on this idea, drogue logs were eventually superseded by towed rotators, which had the advantage of recording the distance travelled.

The main requirement of a drogue log is that it tows smoothly beneath the wake, for once the drogue breaks the surface, readings become erratic and unreliable. This is how to make a very simple log which is capable of quite reliable results. It can be accurate enough for checking the effects of sail adjustments, and may also be used at anchor or a mooring to check the strength of the current. The device is easy to construct but requires testing and calibrating; tasks which younger members of your crew may enjoy.

Materials

- One set of kitchen scales or angler scales for measuring up to 3 kilos (6.5 lb)

- 12 metres of 8mm polyester line

- A wooden frame or base to support the scales

Instructions

A search around bargain stores, boot sales, or even the kitchen should produce an inexpensive set of scales not unlike the one in

the photograph on the left. Having removed any pan or container from its support, bolt a short arm to the support as shown. Secure the scales in a suitable wooden frame, and connect a bridle to the arm. Ensure that the bridle can move without being obstructed. As an alternative, use a set of simple fishing scales (right).

An 8-plait polyester is ideal for the log line because it absorbs water and provides a natural drag effect. At the end of the line make an obstruction. This could be a number of turns in the rough shape of a ball or, if you want it to look a little more decorative, a monkey's fist which you will find in any good book of knots and splices.

Now attach the other end of the line to the bridle using a bowline and secure the frame containing the scales to a suitable place in the cockpit. Finally, measure and place a mark on the line at a point that will be six metres (20ft) from your stern when the log is streamed. Your drogue log is now ready for sea trials so heave it overboard.

If the end of the line surfaces before maximum speed is reached, attach a small weight (200–400g) to the line about one metre from the monkey's fist. Should the scales oscillate, make sure that the supporting frame is attached securely to the boat. You may wish to experiment with different drogue shapes and materials, and different lengths and types of line.

To calibrate the scale

A craft sailing at 1 knot covers 6 metres (20ft) in 12 seconds. So by timing the passage of a surface object (bubbles, seaweed, flotsam etc) from the stern to the 6-metre mark on the line, speed can be measured quite accurately. After several readings have been taken at different speeds, the dial can be be marked up in knots.

Time in seconds	Speed in knots
12	1
6	2
4	3
3	4
2	6
1.5	8
1	12

Having attached the log line to the bridle, firmly secure the tail end to your craft in such a way that it doesn't interfere with the operation of the scales. Then, if you have the misfortune to fall overboard, you'll appreciate just how versatile your drogue log can be.

An acoustic log

The problem. Night is falling and you are eager to get home, but the wind has dropped and your boat is just about making headway. The diesel engine has an airlock. You fuss around with the sails and the tiller, and peer into the darkness for any small improvement in speed.

The solution. Tie a shackle pin to the end of some whipping twine and drop it over the side. Hold the spool or the twine itself against your ear and a sound like a wasp buzzing will be heard, This device is very sensitive to small movements below the surface, and the sound will rise in frequency and volume as the boat's speed increases.

Singlehander

A protractor for knee-top navigation

I don't know how I managed without one.
Capt. W. Bligh

Singlehander is a simple home-made protractor for checking bearings or courses from a chart. It's an ideal device on a small boat where knee-top navigation in the cockpit is the norm and plotters or parallel rules are awkward to handle. It's designed to provide a rapid and accurate check on the true course to be steered, or the true bearing between two objects, and it achieves this by using any vertical or horizontal lines that may be printed on the chart. The protractor consists of an A4 sheet of acetate on which are printed several parallel lines, each with an arrowhead, and a compass rose with an inner and outer scale. There are no extraneous marks or features such as compass variation boxes, reciprocal bearings, tide information, chart scales, movable arms, instructions in several foreign languages and similar clutter to confuse the navigator.

Making it

Enlarge and photocopy the diagram from page 40 onto a sheet of clear acetate and place it inside a transparent plastic folder for protection.

Using it

The device is laid on the chart so that one of the parallel lines coincides exactly with the desired course or bearing between two objects. Singlehander is slid up or down this bearing until the centre of the compass rose coincides with a line of latitude or longitude (or other horizontal or vertical lines printed on the chart). The true bearing is found where the chart line cuts the compass scale. In the two examples which follow, the red line represents the course or bearing to be checked and the blue line represents a horizontal or vertical line on the chart.

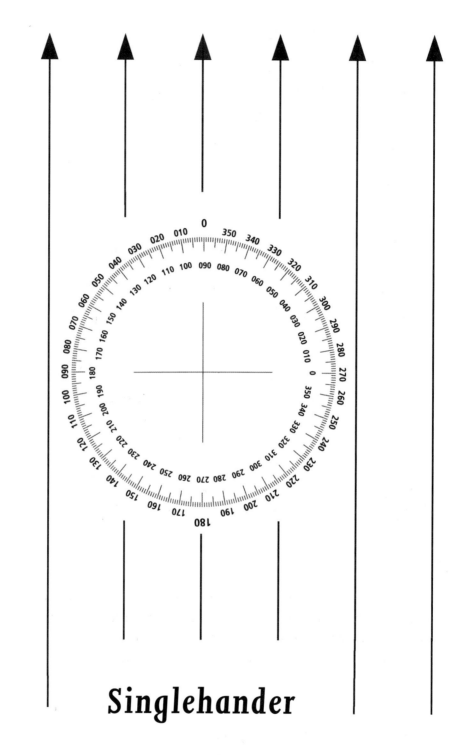

Singlehander

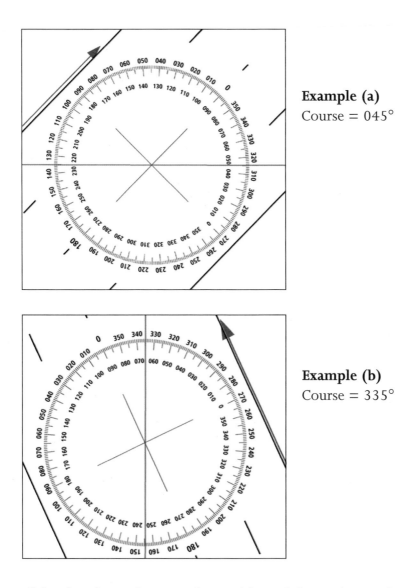

Example (a)
Course = 045°

Example (b)
Course = 335°

If the chart line is horizontal as in (a), read the course on the inner scale. If the chart line is vertical as in (b), read it on the outer scale. Note that both scales are graded in an anti-clockwise direction. Forget this and you could be as much as 10° off course.

The magic of 6°

I once worked aboard a rusty trampship which steamed around the South Pacific at a steady ten knots. For navigation equipment, we had little more than a sextant, chronometer and magnetic compass, but at ten knots there was plenty of time to find our position. At this speed, we had a very simple and effective method of adjusting the course to counter the effects of any tides and currents. It is easily adapted for use on slower sailing craft, and may also be used to calculate the distance off various objects. It is based on the figure of 6° and this is how it works.

Counteracting a current

At 10 knots, if there is a cross-current of 1 knot, the course is adjusted by 6° in the direction from which the current flows. If the cross-current is 2 knots, the course is adjusted by 12° (2 × 6°). If the cross-current is 3 knots, the adjustment is 18° (3 × 6°), and so on. Just how well these figures match up to the correct adjustments is shown in the table below which assumes a boat speed of 10 knots.

Cross-current rate (in knots)	Correction to maintain course	6° shortcut
1	5.7°	6°
2	11.5°	12°
3	17.5°	18°
4	23.6°	24°
5	30.0°	30°
6	36.9°	36°

Though a small craft is unlikely to make ten knots, the basic principle is the same. Calculate the current as a percentage of the boat's speed and for each 10% allow an adjustment of 6°. For example, a 2-knot cross-current on a craft making 5 knots equals 40% of the boat's speed. The course adjustment is 4 × 6° = 24°. The procedure works well up to a cross-current rate of 60%; thereafter, the system, and possibly the boat, are overwhelmed by the strength of the current.

But what if the current is on the bow or on the quarter? The influence is not as strong as that of a cross-current and the correction is reduced to 4°. So, for a 2-knot bow or quarter current on a craft making 5 knots, the adjustment is 4 × 4° = 16°. Note that the adjustment is the same for bow or quarter current as the vector diagrams below show. The only difference is that the current speeds up the boat on the quarter and slows it down on the bow.

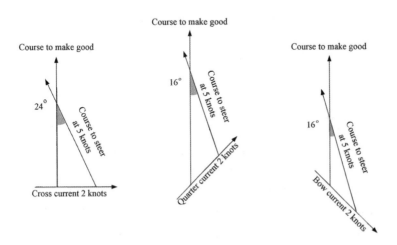

Estimating current strength and direction is not an exact science so these two figures of 6° and 4° should be sufficient for most situations. On a sailing boat, a further adjustment for leeway may be necessary to maintain the intended course. The next time you see a current problem solved by vector solution in a magazine or textbook, try out this simplified method and see how closely it matches the correct solution.

Estimating the distance off

The 6° procedure with a multiplier of ten provides a handy way of estimating your distance from an object with a known height. On a small craft it is suitable for distances up to about four miles, for beyond that distance the base of the object would be obscured by the horizon.

For example, when an object with a height above sea level of 100 metres is 6° above the horizon, it is approximately 1,000 metres away (100 metres × 10).

Working out the distance off for other angles is quite easy as long as you remember the inverse relationship between 6° and the multiplier of 10. For example, at 3° the multiplier of 10 is doubled to 20 so the distance off in the example is 2,000 metres. At 12° the multiplier of 10 is halved to 5 so the distance off is 500 metres.

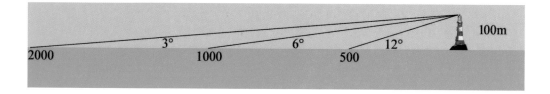

This procedure for estimating the distance off from a vertical height may also be used horizontally when the width of an object, or the distance between two equidistant objects, is known or can be obtained from a chart.

Some quick ways of estimating 6°

The blink of an eye. Hold out a finger at arm's length and line it up on an object with your right eye. Switch to your left eye and the finger will appear to have moved clockwise through a horizontal angle of 6°. This is a typical figure but it is worth checking the angular shift of your wink with the help of a sextant. This is also a useful trick for estimating leeway from your wake.

A finger sextant. Three fingers together at arm's length will usually cover an angle of about 6°. Once again, check out your own angle with a sextant.

Binoculars. Many binoculars have a field of vision in the region of 6°.

A Kamal. The Kamal is one of the oldest angle measuring devices and was used by Arab navigators to cross the Indian Ocean. It is very efficient at measuring small angles and consists of a small board with a knotted line passing through a hole drilled in the centre of the board. A kamal for measuring 6° is made by drilling a small hole in a piece of hardwood 6cm × 6cm. Take a length of line and tie an overhand knot at

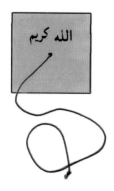

one end. Pull the other end of the line through the hole until the knot
is hard against the board. Tie another knot in the the line approximately
57cm from the board. When this knot is placed in or close to your
mouth and the line held taut, the kamal will cover an angle of 6°.
A kamal may be adapted to measure other angles by extending the
line, adding more knots, or altering the dimensions of the board.

Alcor

The next time you look at the Plough (or Big Dipper), see if you can spot a small star close to the middle star of the handle or tail.

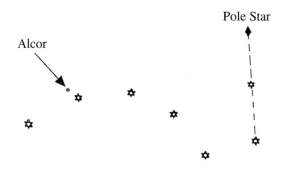

Tradition has it that this star (Alcor) was used as an eyesight test many centuries ago for men joining Arabian armies. The failure rate was high but that probably says more about the popularity of an army career than its value as a sight test. It was certainly used by some sailing ship captains to check if a seaman's vision was good enough for steering by night.

Nothing to do with Alcor, but do you ever go below to check something on the chart and find you have mislaid your reading glasses? Just reverse your binoculars (they're hanging around your neck) and peer down through one of the object lenses. With the eyepiece close to the chart, you will have an excellent magnifier.

Spice jar navigation lights

Under the international collision regulations, the lighting requirements for small craft are remarkably casual and are often reflected in the quality of the equipment fitted. For example, instead of sidelights and a stern light, a sailing vessel of less than seven metres in length is only required to have an electric torch or lighted lantern showing a white light. Even when under power and not exceeding seven knots, the same craft need only display an all-round white light. The red and green sidelights required by larger vessels need only be displayed if practicable. Weaving a four-tonner through a crowded mooring whilst waving a small torch sounds like an accident waiting to to happen and the temporary lights described here could lessen the risk of a collision. Under sail, these lights should only be used if there is no risk of their being obscured by the sails.

AN ALL-ROUND MAST-MOUNTED WHITE LIGHT

This is an all-round emergency or temporary navigation light with a difference. Though mounted for'd of the mast, it's visible from every direction. The lamp consists of a 12v 10W bulb sealed in a glass spice jar and a set of clear acetate reflectors. Viewed from astern, the reflections gradually merge into a single strong light. The design is for a mast up to 10cm (4in) diameter. For a larger mast, increase the dimensions accordingly, but the reflector angles must remain the same.

Materials

- Wood: 150mm × 100mm × 10mm (2)
  120mm × 50mm × 10mm
  120mm × 10mm × 10mm

- One 12v 10W bulb and holder

- A length of flex

- A discarded spice jar and lid

- A sheet of clear acetate
  180mm × 150mm × 1mm
  (or thicker)

- Adhesive and fixings

- Varnish or woodstain

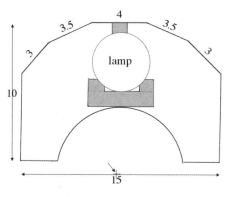

Making the light

Cut out the upper and lower faces as shown above and assemble as shown below. Connect the flex to the lamp holder and feed it through a hole in the spice jar's lid and secure it with an overhand knot. Wrap electrical tape around the lamp holder until it is a snug fit well up

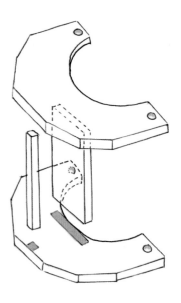

inside the spice jar. For waterproofing, smear the inside of the lid with grease or plumbers mait and screw it on the spice jar. Secure the jar in the frame with the help of two small supports which may be removed to permit removal of the lamp. Cut five strips of acetate and secure them to the front of the frame with brass screws. The acetate in the lamp shown in the photograph came from an unwanted photoframe. Drill four holes in the frame and through them attach short lines for lashing the device to the mast. In normal conditions, the white light is visible from 2 miles and the reflected image from 1 to 1.5 miles. A 5W or a 2.2W bulb will lessen drain on the battery but will reduce the light's visibility.

COMBINED SIDELIGHTS LAMP

Once again, the design is for a mast up to 10cm (4in) diameter.

Materials

- Wood: 150mm × 100min × 10mm (2)
  120mm × 100mm × 10mm
  120mm × 60mm × 10mm

- One 12v 10W bulb and holder

- A length of flex

- A discarded spice jar and lid

- Flexible red and green acetate

- Some red and green paint

- Adhesive and fixings

- Varnish or woodstain

Making the sidelights

Cut the wooden frame and assemble as shown. Paint the two halves in the appropriate colours. Assemble the lamp as described above. Cut several strips of coloured acetate to fit inside the spice jar so that the green acetate covers 200° and the red acetate 160°. This will stop the red light, which has a tendency to dominate, from leaking into the green section. The acetate in the lamp shown came from some OHP slides. Secure the lamp inside the frame with two removable supports. Drill two holes in the frame and through them attach a short line for lashing the device to the mast. Either light will be visible over an arc of 112.5° up to a distance of 1 to 1.5 miles.

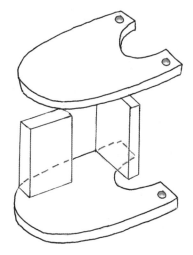

Spice jar lamps may also be used to make a stern light or a simple anchor light. The light shown here has been working for almost 20 years.

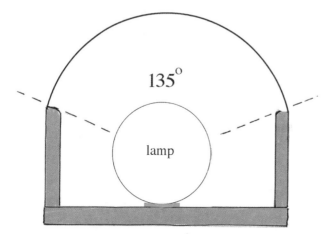

A ready-made heliograph

A heliograph is a mirror with a small hole which is used to attract attention by flashes of sunlight. One way of aiming a heliograph is to extend an arm and an upright finger in the required direction of the signal. Then, by looking through a hole in the centre of the mirror, aim the sun's reflection on the finger tip and the signal will be seen where it is required. You may already have a ready-made supply of heliographs aboard. Use one of the shiny CDs that are strung around the rigging to discourage seabirds from discharging their cargo of guano.

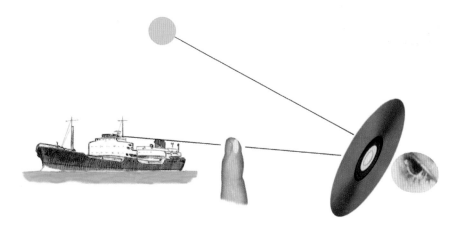

A weekend sailor's logbook

Most commercially produced logbooks look pretty dull and pointless for the average weekend sailing trip. Here is an alternative, which requires a little preparation but which will eventually provide an unusual souvenir of your voyages, however modest they may be. The logbook is unique because you tailor the pages according to the kind of sailing trips you make and the age and interests of the crew. The loose-leaf pages are prepared earlier with ideas from sailing books or magazines and are completed as the voyage unfolds. At the end of the season they can be combined in a folder. Here are some of the main headings:

- Information about the yacht and the crew
- The dates of the voyage and places visited
- Information about the tide and the weather
- Navigation and voyage notes
- Replacement stores required and repairs to be made

Other features could include:

- A voyage motto
- A recipe
- A cartoon
- A puzzle or riddle
- A boating tip
- A photo or sketch
- The lyrics of a song
- An amusing incident
- A close mishap

A logbook like this will keep younger members of the crew interested and involved in what is happening and they will enjoy helping to complete it.

Log

Yacht: Shimmering   **Voyage number:** 12   **Date**: 4 August 2004
From: Osea Island   **To**: Rowhedge Quay
Voyage motto: 'A place for everything and everything in its place!'

Crew members and duties

Teresa:	Skipper
Mark:	Catering and radio
Helen:	Sail trimming, soundings
Jack:	Dinghy, lookout, cabin-boy

Wind, tide and weather

Wind direction and speed:	South-west, force 3 to 4
State of sea:	Slight
Visibility:	Good
Next high tide:	2050 at Southend
Height:	5.4m
Barometer:	1012 steady/rising/falling
Weather forecast:	Wind increasing from the west in the next 24 hours

Navigation notes

Course	Distance	Waypoint	Time	Sounding
080	1	Thirstlet	1520	4
050	3	Naas	1630	6
090	3.5	Cocum	1750	1
030	2	No.13	1820	3
320	3	No.15	1920	5
002	1.5	No.19	1950	3
Various	2.5	Rowhedge	2040	6

Date and time of arrival:	4 August 2004, 2040hrs
Distance covered:	16.5
Average speed	3kn
Repairs required:	Boathook broken, batten pocket torn in mainsail
Stores required:	Two-stroke oil, coffee, some painkillers

Voyage notes

Shimmering ran aground 1 mile NE of the Cocum Hills – remains of a nearby wreck still visible at low water. Reported abandoned dinghy off Sandy Point to Coastguard.

Useful tip

Poke a small hole in the centre of a large car sponge. Push it down the handle of a deck scrubber until it rests on the head. One dip into the bucket, river or ocean will keep the bristles replenished saving time and energy.

Galley gruel: Spanish Armada omelette

Fry pieces of cooked potato, chopped onion, bacon and tomato etc. Beat four eggs and pour over the contents of the pan. When risen, grill until brown. Serve with french bread and salad. Wash down with a flagon of amber nectar.

Song chest

Wild Rover

I've been a wild rover for many a year,
and I spent all my money on whisky and beer.
But now I'm returning with gold in great store,
And I never will play the wild rover no more.
And it's no nay never, no nay never no more
Will I play the wild rover, no nay never no more.

All for me grog

And it's all for me grog, me jolly jolly grog
All for me beer and tobacco.
Well I spent all me tin on ladies fond of gin
And across the western ocean I must wander.

Memory bank

Anchored off Osea, 3 August 2004

Four moorings and a fiasco

Mooring n. *a place of safety where a vessel is secured by chain or rope.*

Some years after leaving the Merchant Navy, I recalled a boyhood ambition to own a sailing ship and explore the South Seas. As I stared wearily past my reflection on a crowded train from work, I heard surf breaking over a reef and pictured myself landing on some flowering coral shore and surrounded by beautiful maidens. All I asked was 'a tall ship and a star to steer her by'. By the time I got home, I had made up my mind to buy a boat, learn the ropes, and set sail for Paradise. Unfortunately, the great adventure did not unfold in quite the way that I had anticipated.

I searched for my dream ship with an abundance of optimism matched only by my ignorance. After exploring several boatyards and marinas, I was much taken by *Osmosis*, a simple but rugged craft named, I assumed, after some ancient Egyptian god; very possibly a god of the sea. This seemed to be confirmed when the owner nudged me and with a knowing wink said 'Tempting fate, eh?' Indeed, *Osmosis* may have been cursed but not by any form of wet rot which her name, apparently, implied. After a trial sail, and having accepted my first offer, he handed over a large bunch of keys. 'This one will get you into the clubhouse at B. This one usually unlocks the showers at M. This opens the yard gates at D.' etc.

'And what about the keys to the boat?' I asked as he hurried away up the pontoon.

'Oh nobody will want to pinch that,' was his brief reply. He was leaving the country to open an underwater diving school in the Canary Islands. Little did I know that with the passage of time I was to envy his occupational skills. Later, I sat in the cabin and studied the boat's papers. She was registered under a different name, and had six previous owners: all were 'company directors' and none had kept her for more than two seasons. Heartened by their experiences in this modest yacht they had probably upgraded to something more in keeping with their status. Reassured by these thoughts, I spent several challenging hours starting the engine.

I liked the small marina in which *Osmosis* lay and wrote to the manager expressing an interest in retaining the berth. His reply was swift and blunt. The previous owner had left several unpaid bills and, as the new owner, these were now my responsibility. Under marine lien, certain debts remained with a vessel and he would have no hesitation in impounding the yacht if they were not paid immediately.

I was stunned, and pictured a writ being nailed to the mast and steel barges forming a menacing blockade. Fortunately, a friend had advised the insertion of the phrase 'free of all encumbrances' in the bill of sale so I wrote a stern letter to the previous owner reminding him of his responsibilities. Would this be sufficient? I stared doubtfully at the large bunch of unofficial keys which I had inherited and planned our escape. Then more unfinished business at other yards came to light and it was clear that something more drastic was required. Armed with a bowsprit and fittings, an unusual boom support, some quick-drying deck paint and a pair of temporary name boards, I sneaked into the yard under cover of darkness. At dawn, the pea-green cutter *Little Owl* slipped quietly from the marina and out to sea in search of new and distant cruising grounds. On reflection, it had been a useful experience. For the first (and possibly the last) time in my life, I had purchased a cranse iron (galvanised) and attached a bobstay. I had also discovered the meaning of lien.

We wintered in a canal that was choked with waterlogged sailing craft and abandoned dreams. As space was limited, *Osmosis* was forced to moor alongside a large yacht, the owner of which lived in America. After a few weeks, I noticed that water was gradually seeping into the cockpit of his yacht and lapping around the duckboards leading to the cabin. Thereafter, on my weekly visit to the canal, I manned the pumps vigorously and kept her reasonably dry and afloat. It seemed the right thing to do – 'hands across the sea' and all that.

One pleasant afternoon, as I sat on *Osmosis* enjoying the pale winter sun, a man appeared on the towpath. In a hectoring voice, he reprimanded me for my matching pair of Michelin fenders, my overtight mooring lines and my muddy footprints. It was the yacht's owner recently returned from the colonies. Maintaining a dignified silence, I slipped my lines and managed to find another mooring further up the canal. Call it mean-spirited if you will, but when we passed a little later on the towpath, I couldn't bring myself to tell him about his leak. Anyway, it had been a useful experience and I had some helpful tips on the etiquette of rafting up.

Spring beckoned. I joined a sailing club and received an invitation to a pre-season meeting. Impressed by pompous titles such as 'commodore' and the like, I wore a smart blazer with a Merchant Navy tie and, during the 50 miles drive to the coast, rehearsed a short acceptance speech. The members assembled in the rain on a drab sea wall overlooking a featureless estuary. The vice-commodore (senior) explained to the newcomers that the club had no premises (burnt down), no social activities (secretary resigned), and no newsletter (nothing to report), but it had a shed, a slipway and spare moorings, all of which needed urgent maintenance. Suitably attired for work, the others set about their tasks with enthusiasm. Prancing about like a Boat Show rep in the mud, I must have looked a complete idiot. Anyway, *Osmosis* was allocated a buoy close to a beach which was overlooked by a large holiday caravan site. Viewed from the fish and chip kiosk, she looked isolated and vulnerable.

A month later, I arrived at the slipway in time to see a gang of kids boarding and ransacking my beloved craft. They had already taken the binoculars, fire extinguisher, clock, torch, compass, lamps, radio and charts, and were returning for anything else on which they could lay their hands. The vice-commodore (junior) and I rowed out stealthily to apprehend them, but inexplicably, as we rounded the stern, he shouted out in anger. They immediately dived overboard and made for the shore, leaving behind a large dinghy, which he deflated. Several club members trawled through the caravan site and recovered most of my belongings whilst angry parents unleashed their wrath on the culprits. I was grateful for the help the club had given but decided to quit the mooring on the ebb tide. Sailing past a spit of land, I noticed the gang of mudlarks gesticulating and shouting. Assuming they were hurling abuse, I ignored them and sailed on imperiously. Several hours later, I discovered a large dinghy in the forecabin. All in all it was a useful experience and helped to clarify the role of a yacht club's vice-commodore.

Summer was slipping by with still no sign of a permanent parking place. In makeshift havens, *Osmosis* yearned to be free and persistently dragged her anchor. One memorable night, a borrowed mooring buoy parted company with its cable and the ebb tide carried the three of us gently down the estuary and out to sea. Then a call came from a boatyard which had a spare mooring alongside a jetty. 'Can you bring her in next Friday? It would be ... er ... more convenient.' I arrived on time to discover that alongside meant bow lines to the jetty, stern lines to mooring buoys, and breast lines to nearby craft. But worse was to follow. My arrival had been conveniently timed to coincide with an exceptionally high tide. At most other tides, Osmosis squatted in the mud like a trussed-up duck and refused to budge. Even when she was afloat, it took a well-organised operation with the dinghy to release her without fouling a spider's web of lines from other boats. More often than not, I gave up in despair and sat aboard strumming my ukelele and dreaming of Tahiti. Although I hadn't started baying at full moon, things were moving in that direction, so I left – but with some reluctance, for it was a friendly place and the staff were ever helpful and considerate. They even sent me a farewell card with their best wishes. However, it had been a useful experience: my knowledge of tides had increased considerably and I now had a clearer perception of spring tides and what it meant to be neaped.

It was autumn once more. Osmosis sat snugly in a mudberth at the edge of some saltings. As the tide rose, an armada of small boats emerged from the mud and bobbed around on the top of the marshes. When the tide fell, the boats gradually disappeared from sight leaving a forest of masts to mark their resting place. On a misty morning, it was a mysterious and fascinating sight: the perfect mooring in harmony with nature. All was serene until that fateful day when, unbeknown to me, the yard made some changes to my mooring stage and snagged my lines. Trapped by her stern on a flood tide, Osmosis suffered what the surveyor's report called 'a severe ingress of sea water', i.e. she sank. At high tide, only the wooden mast, guarded by a lone seagull, was visible. It seemed the last straw, particularly when the yard refused to accept any responsibility and its insurers accused me of negligence. Fortunately, my insurers were not fobbed off so easily. They pursued the case with vigour to the door of the court and the other side conceded defeat. All the costs were recovered including some extra compensation for 'loss of pleasure' – a doubtful bonus but one that was gratefully accepted. By and large it had been a useful experience for it had helped me to discover, not only the value of adequate marine insurance, but two extra seacocks. Also, in a brief moment of frustration, I had found another use for that intriguing word ingress.

Raised and restored, Osmosis returned to the mooring. It had been a long season and we were both tired of running. With winter approaching, it was a time to reflect on all those valuable experiences and to face the new season with renewed optimism. Hopefully, there would be more useful lessons and less useless moorings. The South Seas might have to wait, but at least I could now bluff my way in sailing with a whole new vocabulary.

Originally published in **Practical Boat Owner**, August 2003

Threefold puzzle

Although the threefold purchase is not often seen on small sailing craft, it can often be found around boatyards and on large sailing ships where its extra power is invaluable. Reeving a threefold purchase appears a tricky job, but if the blocks are placed correctly, it is much easier than it looks. Have a go at working it out on the sketch here. It may help if you imagine how the blocks appear when viewed from above. Reeve the fall of the rope through the middle sheave of the upper block to start with. The solution is on page 145.

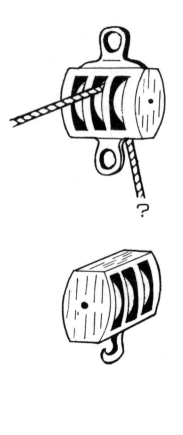

A hand leadline

A hand leadline is rarely found aboard a modern yacht but it's a really useful piece of equipment. Not only can it be used to check the depth of water if the depth sounder fails, but it can also help to identify the

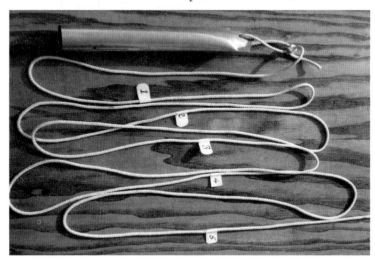

nature of the seabed. In a situation where there is little room to manoeuvre a larger craft, soundings can be taken from the ship's dinghy. This version, which weighs about 7lb, was constructed with the following materials:

- 12 metres of 4mm non-stretch line

- A large metal pipe (a rotating washing-line support)

- A quantity of lead shot and scrap lead

- Strips of material and a waterproof marker

- Chemical metal filler

Construction

The sinker is crammed with an assortment of lead pieces and sealed at the bottom with chemical metal. The bottom of the sinker has an indentation into which is pressed some seacock grease or soft putty (see photo). This brings up a small amount of gravel,

mud or sand etc to help you check the nature of the seabed. To save making a heavy sinker, a folded grapnel anchor could be used instead.

Traditionally, hand leadlines were marked at various fathoms with strips of leather, bunting, linen, etc. The idea of using different materials was to enable the leadsman to take soundings in the dark and feel the depth from the nature of the material. Presumably, this

was useful when a ship was approaching a hostile shore and maintaining a blackout. On this leadline, however, each metre is marked by a strip of cloth stitched to the line and indicating the depth from the top of the sinker. Measuring from the top of the sinker provides a small safety margin.

I once saw a leadline used as an alarm clock in a mudberth. The line was attached to some pan lids hanging from the boom. The sinker rested in the mud and, when the tide rose, the pans clashed together like cymbals. I was a bit doubtful about this arrangement, until it woke me at some unearthly hour.

Reading the sea

For this project, no special materials or tools are required though a camera with a zoom lens might come in handy. All you need is a fairly calm day at anchor, your powers of observation and a great deal of patience. The purpose of the exercise is to explore the ways in which the early Pacific navigators read the current from the surface of the sea.

Some basics

The navigator often wishes to take advantage of, or avoid, the current, but how easy is it to detect? A wake of bubbles will stream from a buoy or other moored object in the direction of the current and, unless the wind is very strong, an anchored yacht will point up to it. Sometimes, as a current flows through water, it may be seen deflecting marine plants or dragging a line of debris at its edge. But what if there

are no physical objects to guide you? Even when the water is free of obstructions, the current can be seen working with or against the wind through the behaviour of waves. If the wind is against the current, the faces of the waves become short and steep and the sea becomes choppy. If the wind is with the current, the waves are much smoother and longer. These effects are often seen on a windy day in an estuary or a river when the tide is ebbing or flowing, but may also be observed on calm days with only a light wind.

The photo at the top of the page opposite was taken when both wind and current were approaching the camera.

As the wind reaches the faster current in the foreground, it meets less resistance and the water's surface is relatively smooth. In the slower current where the boats are moored, there is more resistance to the wind and the surface is broken. When the tide changes, the faster current will offer more resistance and the effect will be reversed: a rougher surface with sharper crests will replace the smooth one.

Sailing against the wind and current, you may be tempted to avoid the smooth water to save time, but keep an eye on your soundings as stronger currents usually indicate deeper water. Sometimes, of course, that smooth patch may just be an oil slick.

Wind and current in the open sea

But how can you detect a current when you are out on the open sea? Unless you pass through a patch of rough and confused water where two currents meet, you would probably not know of its existence. You could, of course, heave to and switch on the GPS, but that's cheating. Another solution may be found in the knowledge and skills developed by the ancient Pacific navigators. They knew, for example, that when they entered a strong current there was often a change in the colour of the sea, or in its temperature and that of the surrounding air. When the wind increased, these early navigators studied the whitecaps on the wave crests. If the caps tumbled over gently and seethed into a long streak, the current was running with the wind. If the caps peaked abruptly, fell and were drawn back to windward, the current was flowing against the wind.

With weaker currents, these changes were harder to detect, so in a gentle swell with light winds, they studied the ripples formed by the wind on the surface of the sea. As a light breeze blows across smooth water, it stretches the surface into small wavelets with rounded crests and v-shaped troughs. These are known as capillary waves and, resisted by surface tension, they soon disappear. If the wind's speed increases, larger or gravity waves are formed but capillary waves may still be seen running ahead of the crests. With the current, they ripple lazily downwind and fade. Opposing the current, they decelerate, contract and are more persistent. In a cross-current, they travel at different angles and collide with each other. When the opportunity arises, see if you can find them and compare their appearance at different stages of the tide.

Reading the ripples takes patience and practice because they can occur when waves collide, and there are other surface disturbances too, but why not check it out and see if it works for you.

Detecting a weaker, deep current

Here is another trick to try out when you are becalmed in deep water. Drop the end of a weighted line over the side and, after a few minutes, watch the direction in which the line streams as it disappears into the depths. Generally, currents below the surface are weaker and, sometimes, a boat will drag the line in the direction of the stronger current. Today's oceanographers use sonar and lasar beams to establish the profiles of currents at different depths, but two hundred years ago, ships' captains relied on an iron kettle from the galley attached to a long line.

Self-steering

Fixed helm

Some form of self-steering system, if only of a temporary nature, can be a great boon to the singlehanded sailor. It releases the helmsman for other tasks, to have a rest or prepare a meal and so on.

In a steady breeze, a well-balanced boat with a little weather helm will often sail itself to windward with nothing more than a lashed tiller. Sailing to windward, a boat heels more readily but the heeling has a stabilising function. If the boat bears away, it heels and luffs up to wind: if it luffs up to wind, it heels less and bears away again.

Sailing downwind, however, heeling no longer provides this kind of stability. If the boat bears away, it heels less and having a fixed helm may continue bearing away until it gybes. If it luffs up to wind and heels, it may continue luffing up until it is sailing to windward. In addition, a boat with a locked helm has no way of compensating for variations in wind strength so the method is usually limited to windward sailing in a steady wind.

A couple of tips on fixed-helm steering from experts. On a windward beat, if you've tried the lashed tiller approach with limited success than back-wind the main a little by trimming the headsail flatter. Bearing away on the headsail and luffing up on the main, the boat will then weave a course within a few degrees either side of a close reach. On a broad reach or a run, if the boat keeps luffing up, adjust the sail plan to reduce any excessive weather helm and, if feasible, bend a small jib to a jib pole or makeshift bowsprit.

Sheet-to-tiller

Another inexpensive option is what is generally known as sheet-to-tiller steering and it has been used successfully in many ocean crossings. The system is ideal for a well-balanced yacht with a small amount of weather helm. Usually, a line from the jib, a backed storm sail or the mainsail is led through one or more blocks to the weather side of the tiller and the other side of the tiller is restrained by one or more lengths of shock cord or surgical tubing. When the wind freshens, the boat heels and starts to head up to the wind – the extra tension in the sheet draws the tiller to windward and the boat bears away. When the wind eases, the shock cord returns the tiller to its normal position, at which point it should relax.

The system should work on most points of sailing, but many sheet-to-tiller sailors find that it works better upwind than downwind. A number of reasons are offered for this. A reduction in the apparent wind speed means less power for the system, weather helm increases and the effects of heeling are different. Nevertheless, it can be made to work – it just takes more time to find the right adjustments. In a small yacht, the distribution of weight can make a considerable difference to self-steering, so resist the tendency to admire your efforts from the bows. Furthermore, if you fall overboard, then, despite the loss of weight, your boat may sail off without you, so sit tight and enjoy it.

Tiller sail

My tiller sail started life as a joke intended for the internet, but I tried it out and was surprised by the results. It is nothing more that a small triangular sail attached by a spar to an adjustable telescopic pole. The pole is lashed to the tiller and extended so that the sail looks like a fin behind the boat. By adjusting the pole, the sail can be extended, retracted or feathered. A length of bungee or shock cord runs from the tiller to the leeward coaming, but there are no sheets from the sails, or cat's cradle of lines and blocks, so the cockpit remains fairly clear.

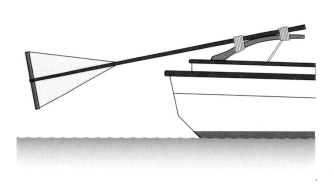

How does it work? When the

wind freshens, the tiller sail is immediately drawn to leeward and pushes the tiller to windward slightly which cancels out the boat's tendency to heel and luff up to wind. When the wind eases, the bungee cord returns the tiller to its original setting. Downwind, if weather helm increases, the tiller sail is assisted by some bungee cord added

to the windward side of the tiller. Though a part of the sail plan, this small sail continually fences with the tiller and keeps the boat on course throughout the gusts.

1912

Wrecked and stranded on this iceberg
Steady lads and do not fear,
I have sent an SOS
and know that help will soon be here.

Wrecked and stranded on this iceberg
Steady lads and don't despair,
We shall soon be wrapped in blankets
and a change of underwear.

Wrecked and stranded on this iceberg
Steady lads, let spirits rise,
Compared to Newport in the rain,
Why this place is paradise!

Wrecked and stranded on this iceberg
Steady lads and do not panic
To our rescue comes a ship,
Oh praise the Lord boys it's Titanic!

Crunch!

Wrecked and stranded on this iceberg
Steady lads, without a moon,
They had difficulty docking,
She'll be back again quite soon.

Sun navigation in a nutshell

In an old Hornblower film, our hero draped himself elegantly against the shrouds, pointed a sextant at the sun and calmly read out the ship's latitude and longitude. Though it looked authentic, it was complete nonsense because navigators do not find their position from a single observation of the sun or any other heavenly body. A single observation can only provide what is known as a position line along which the ship is situated. The position line always runs at right angles to the direction of the observed body and two or more position lines are required to fix the ship's position. The notes which follow refer specifically to the sun but much of what is written applies when navigating by the moon, the planets and the stars.

Finding your position line

To find your position line, two pieces of information are essential. The first is the position on earth that lies directly below the sun at the time of the observation and the second is your distance from that position.

1. The sun's earth position is found with the help of an almanac. Its latitude is reported as being so many degrees north or south of the equator and is called the sun's declination. The sun's longitude, however, is not described as being so many degrees east or west of Greenwich. It is always west of Greenwich and is referred to as the sun's Greenwich hour angle (GHA). So if the sun has a GHA of 300° its longitude is 60° east of Greenwich.

2. The distance from your position to the sun's earth position is exactly the same as the angle from directly above your head to the sun. In practice, this is impossible to measure accurately, so the angle between the horizon and the sun is measured instead. Having been corrected for certain errors and subtracted from 90°, the result is known as the zenith distance.

Zenith distance = 90° - sun's altitude

The ease with which you use the zenith distance to plot the position line will depend on the direction of the sun. If the sun is due north or south, your position line will be a line of latitude.

This is very easy to calculate and is why navigators take a sight of the sun at local noon. You can also find your longitude by timing when the sun is exactly due south (or north) and checking its GHA in the almanac. In practice, however, it is quite a challenge to time the sun's transit accurately so the result would only be a rough guide to your longitude.

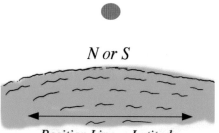

N or S

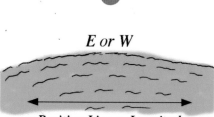

Position Line = Latitude

Because the position line is at right angles to the sun, you can find your longitude by observing the sun when it is due east or west. This procedure is not very complicated but the sun will only cross your east–west line if it is in the same hemisphere as your latitude, and nearer the equator.

E or W

Position Line = Longitude

When the sun is bearing in other directions, the procedure to find the position line is more complex and requires an estimate of your latitude and longitude. As mentioned earlier, a ship's position is found by combining two or more position lines. If only the sun is available, then two observations several hours apart will be required. The ship's position is where the two position lines cross, but an adjustment to the position of the first line will be required if the ship has moved between the two observations.

An outline of the three procedures follows and the calculations are performed using an inexpensive scientific calculator. But first, look at the corrections which may need to be made to angles measured with a sextant.

Sextant corrections

There may be errors on the sextant itself and the most common is index error. If the sextant is measuring too high, the index error must be deducted. If it is measuring too low, the index error must be added. After index error, the main corrections are for:

1. Height of eye above sea level. The observed angle increases with height.

2. Semi-diameter. An addition or subtraction depending on whether the sun's lower or upper limb is lowered to the horizon.

3. Atmospheric refraction, which makes the sun appear higher than it is, particularly at lower altitudes.

Height of eye (subtract)		Sun's semi-diameter		Refraction (subtract)	
2m	= 2.5'	Lower limb	= +16'	0°	= 33'
3m	= 3'	Upper limb	= −16'	1°	= 25'
4m	= 3.5'			5°	= 10'
5m	= 4'			10°	= 5'
10m	= 6'			20°	= 2.5'
15m	= 7'			30°	= 2'
20m	= 9'			40°	= 1'

To find your latitude at noon

To find latitude at local noon, measure and correct the sun's altitude when it's due north or due south and look up its declination. Next, convert the sun's altitude to a zenith distance by subtracting it from 90°. The formula for calculating latitude depends on whether the sun, the equator or the observer lies between the other two.

Equator between sun
and observer: Lat = zenith distance − declination

Sun between equator
and observer: Lat = zenith distance + declination

Observer between
equator and sun: Lat = declination − zenith distance

Example

A navigator in the southern hemisphere observes the sun bearing north.

● Sextant altitude of the sun's lower limb = 40°02'

● The sextant has an error on the arc of 2'
   (i.e. it over-measures the angle)

- Height of eye = 3m

- Sun's declination = 12°23' N

Correction

Altitude of the sun's lower limb:	40°02'
Index error (on the arc):	− 02'
Corrected sextant altitude:	40°00'

Other corrections

Height of eye 3m:	− 03'
Semi-diameter:	+ 16'
Refraction:	− 01'
Sun's true altitude (= 40°00' − 03' + 16' − 01'):	40°12'
Sun's zenith distance (= 90° − 40°12'):	49°48'
Observer's latitude (= 49°48' − 12°23'):	**37°25' S**

To find your longitude when the sun is due east or west

When the sun is due east or west, the local hour angle or difference between your longitude and the sun's earth longitude (GHA) is found by this formula:

$$\frac{\cos \text{ sun's altitude}}{\cos \text{ sun's declination}} = \sin \text{ hour angle}$$

Example

On 6 May 2003 at 0745 GMT, the sun was due east at an altitude of 24°59'. The sun's GHA was 302°20' (which is the same as longitude 57°40' east) and its declination was 16°27' N.

$$\frac{\cos 24°59'}{\cos 16°27'} = \frac{.90643}{.95906} = .94511 = \sin 70°55'$$

The observer is 70°55' west of the sun which is in longitude 57°40' E.
70°55' − 57°40' = 13°15'. The observer, therefore, is in longitude
13°15' W.

To find your position line at other times

This poem will guide you through the key stages of plotting a position
line when the sun is neither east/west nor north/south.

First you measure the height of the sun	
and time the sight by GMT.	
Correct for refraction and height of eye,	
sextant error and semi-d.	36°56' at 0957 GMT
Double-check your measurements	
and while you're out there having fun,	
try to take and tidy up	
a compass bearing of the sun.	100°
Now though your lat and long are vague	
just provide an estimation,	Lat 40° N Long 25° W
then use an almanac to find	
the sun's GHA and declination.	GHA 330° Dec 16° N
With GHA and longitude	
take a moment to untangle	
the difference 'tween the sun and you	GHA 330° = Long 30° E
it's called the local hour angle.	30° E to 25° W = LHA of 55°
To use the equation shown below	
you'll need three bits of information:	
your estimated latitude,	
LHA and declination.	Lat 40° LHA 55° Dec 16°
It calculates the sun's true height	
from your estimated base.	Calculated altitude = 36°50'
If there's no match with what you got	
then you are in a different place.	Observed altitude = 36°56'

Your altitude larger? Use the difference
to plot a position nearer the sun.
Your altitude smaller? Then plot the position
the opposite way – that's how it's done.

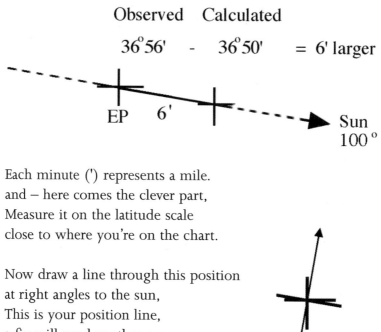

Observed   Calculated

36°56'   -   36°50'   = 6' larger

EP   6'   Sun
             100°

Each minute (') represents a mile.
and – here comes the clever part,
Measure it on the latitude scale
close to where you're on the chart.

Now draw a line through this position
at right angles to the sun,
This is your position line,
a fix will need another one.

The equation:

(cos LHA × cos Lat × cos Dec) ± (sin Lat × sin Dec) = sin Alt

+   when the latitude and declination are the same side of the equator

–   when the latitude and declination are on opposite sides of the
    equator

Example of the equation in action (using the data in the poem)

cos 55° × cos 40° × cos 16° = 0.42236

sin 40° × sin 16° = 0.17717

Lat and Dec are both north

0.42236 + 0.17717 = 0.59953 = sin of 36°50'

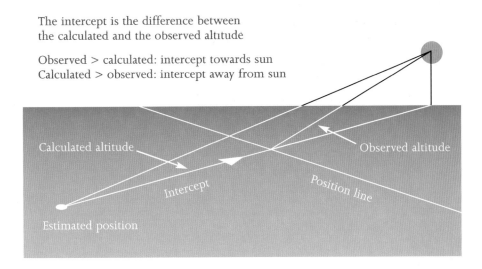

The intercept is the difference between
the calculated and the observed altitude

Observed > calculated: intercept towards sun
Calculated > observed: intercept away from sun

Calculated altitude

Observed altitude

Intercept

Position line

Estimated position

The picture above sums up the procedure.

Finally, here is a useful equation for checking the true bearing of the sun or any other heavenly object:

$$\frac{\sin LHA \times \cos declination}{\cos altitude} = \sin azimuth$$

This calculates the bearing from north or south depending on the object's direction.

Note. In this chapter, the angles were expressed in degrees and minutes. For the simplified and emergency techniques which follow, the angles are generally presented as decimals; so 50°15' becomes 50.25°

A mariner's quadrant

The mariner's quadrant is one of the earliest devices used by navigators to find latitude by measuring the Pole Star's altitude at night, or the sun's altitude at midday. It was adapted from an instrument used by astronomers and surveyors. At night, the observer lined up the Pole Star in the two sights while an assistant read the position of the plumb-line on the degree scale. In the absence of an assistant, the observer pinched the plumb-line against the scale. By day, the quadrant was angled until the light from the sun shone down through both the sighting holes.

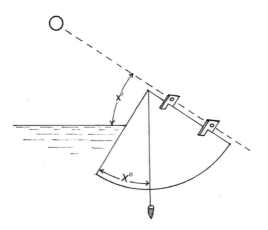

The main advantages of the quadrant were its simple construction and its ability to measure altitudes without reference to the horizon. How it came to be used at sea is something of a mystery as it was only effective in calm conditions. At other times, with the plumb-line swinging uncontrollably, accurate measurements were impossible. Portuguese navigators, however, were quite fond of it and, during voyages along the west coast of Africa, would row ashore to obtain a reliable reading. Perhaps there were other distractions ashore. The mariner's quadrant and the astrolabe – which both used gravity to define their measurements, were eventually replaced by horizon-aligned devices such as the cross-staff and the back-staff.

My first quadrant used a plumb-line and, in a moderate sea, had an error of approximately 1° – equal to 60 miles! Even with the plumb-line replaced by a weighted metal pointer, the results were no better. By trial and error, I developed a quadrant which was more suitable for use at sea. It has the simplicity of the original device, but is designed for use with the sun. The plumb-line is replaced by a small block which casts a shadow on a rim alongside the graduated scale. The quadrant can either be aligned with the real horizon or with an artifical horizon using an in-built spirit level.

How to make the quadrant

Materials required

- One spirit-level bubble unit

- One sheet of wood or fibreboard (MDF) approx 350mm × 350mm × 6mm

- One small block about 1cm square (e.g. Lego), or a pin

- One 0–90° scale with 0.5° graduations

The 90° scale can be copied and enlarged from a suitable protractor – 25cm is about the maximum radius. Glue the scale to the board and

mark its pivotal point. Then cut and peel away the part of the scale that is not required and cover the rest with protective film.

Cut the board to accommodate the radius of the scale plus a further 1.5cm. This additional margin is covered by a rim cut from the spare fibreboard (see photo). The inner edge of the rim is given a slight outward bevel with a suitable file. Glue the rim to the quadrant. Attach the small block so that the upper left corner touches the pivotal point of the scale. Or tap in a pin at the same point.

Cut a window for the spirit-level bubble in the face of the quadrant. The spirit-level bubble unit should fit neatly without protruding. Before gluing it into position, adjust the setting of the bubble by suspending a temporary plumb-line from the small block to 0° on the scale.

Finally paint the inner edge of the rim with white paint and finish the quadrant in woodstain. If you add two edge strips, the quadrant can serve as a drinks tray.

How to use the quadrant

Hold the quadrant so that the upper edge lines up with the horizon or the bubble is level. The sun's rays will pass over the small block and cast a shadow on the rim. With the help of this shadow, you should be able to read the scale to within 0.2° but you may need to cushion the device to steady the bubble.

Variations on the quadrant are presented later, along with some ideas on how they may be used in emergency navigation.

The cross-staff

The cross-staff – also known as the fore-staff or Jacob's staff – served seamen for nearly three hundred years. Though easy to make, it was an awkward instrument to use, and most navigators were glad to abandon it in favour of the back-staff. The cross-staff described here is based on a 16th-century design.

The principles

A cross-staff was used by astronomers and navigators to measure angles between celestial bodies, to determine latitudes, and to measure heights. It consists of a staff about 90cm (3ft) in length along which can slide a cross-piece (or transom) set at right angles to it. To measure the altitude of the sun, one end

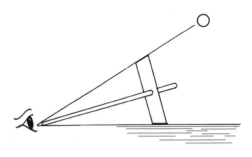

of the staff is held close to the observer's eye, and the cross-piece is adjusted until the upper edge coincides with the sun and the lower edge coincides with the horizon. The altitude is found at a point where the cross-piece cuts a graduated scale on the staff.

Several different cross-pieces, varying in length, are used for measuring small, medium or large angles. Each cross-piece has its own graduated scale printed on the staff for obtaining a direct reading of the altitude in degrees. In other versions, including the one featured in this article, the staff has a single scale indicating the distance from the viewing end of the staff. The altitude is then calculated according to the formula at the end of this chapter.

A cross-staff may also be used for piloting tasks such as measuring distances from an object where its height or width are known. It's also very handy for finding the distance off by doubling the angle on the bow; the initial bearing is observed using half a cross-piece and the second with a full cross-piece.

Despite its simplicity, the cross-staff has several shortcomings. The main problem is that it requires the observer to line up two objects at once – a trying task from the pitching deck of a ship at sea. Another is that the position at which the observer rests the staff against his or her cheekbone may produce variations in the distance from eye to cross-piece. When used for sun sights, the observer has to look directly at the sun – never to be recommended though the glare can be reduced by a smoked-glass shade. In addition, cross-staffs are less reliable for measuring large angles or high altitudes and were rarely used much above 50°.

How to make the cross-staff

Materials

- 1500mm × 21 mm × 21mm hardwood for the staff and cross-piece collars
- 720mm × 60mm × 15mm of wood for the cross-pieces
- One tape measure (80cm)
- One piece of thick glass approx 20mm × 20mm (optional)
- One piece of mirror approx 10mm × 10mm (optional)
- One piece of dowelling approx 50mm × 12mm (optional)

Tools

- A tenon saw or similar
- Wood dowelling bits or drills: 20mm and 12mm (optional)
- A coping saw
- A craft knife
- A flat wood file
- Araldite adhesive
- Glass paper, woodstain and varnish

The staff

Checking that the wood isn't warped, cut 90cm for the staff and sand off any surface irregularities. With a craft knife, cut two sides of a channel about 80cm long and deep enough to accommodate the tape measure. Whittle out the unwanted wood and sand down the surface of the channel.

The cross-pieces

Cut three from the second piece of wood – 12cm, 24cm, and 36cm in length. In the centre of each cross-piece mark out a square 21mm × 21mm, and drill a 20mm hole through the centre of this square. Use a coping saw to remove the corners and carefully file the hole until it's large enough to accommodate the hardwood staff.

From the remaining hardwood, cut some short lengths for a collar and glue them around the hole using simple or mitred joints. The cross-piece should slide smoothly up and down the staff, but the collar will help to reduce any wobble. Bevel the upper and lower edges of the cross-pieces with a 45° slope and shape the sides in whatever style you like.

The scale

Glue the tape measure into the channel with the measurements starting from the eye end. Stained and varnished, your cross-staff is now ready for use. The longer the distance between the cross-piece and your eye, the more accurate will be your measurements, so select whichever cross-piece helps achieve this

Calculating the altitude

To obtain an altitude from a cross-staff, the following formula should be applied:

$$\frac{\text{Half length of cross-piece}}{\text{Distance to observer's eye}} = \text{Tangent of \textbf{half} the altitude}$$

The altitude is found by doubling the angle obtained. For example, if the sun and the horizon touch the ends of a 24cm cross-piece when it's 30cm from the observer's eye, the calculation is as follows:

$12/30 = 0.4 =$ the tangent of $21.8°$

so the altitude $= 43.6°$

A 21st-century cross-staff

I have experimented with a small optical device attached to the viewing end of a cross-staff. This works like a sextant and a shaded image of the sun is lowered to the horizon. Then, without altering the setting of the mirrors, the cross-piece is moved along the staff until the upper and lower edges also appear to meet in the mirrors. The scale is read and the normal calculations made. The device improves the cross-staff's accuracy considerably. In 80 observations, the device had an average error of only $0.05°$ (3'). Unfortunately, it is several centuries too late.

A hi-tech back-staff

In 1595, John Davis, the English explorer and navigator, produced an ingenious device which revolutionised the art of navigation. The Davis quadrant – or back-staff – led the field for nearly 140 years until it was superseded by Hadley's octant, the forerunner of the sextant. A back-staff is reasonably easy to make, and, clamped against a rigid support ashore, is capable of considerable accuracy. However, its use in the pitching cockpit of a small yacht can be a trying experience demanding patience and skill. Denied a sextant by the Bounty mutineers, Captain Bligh used a back-staff to navigate an open boat for over 4,000 miles.

There are many versions of the back-staff, but the one described here is based on a design which was commonly in use during the early part of the 18th century. A few refinements have been added such as a vernier scale and an artificial horizon.

Construction

The back-staff consists of two arcs with a common centre which are mounted on a central staff. The upper arc has a scale spanning 60° and graduated in 10° steps; the lower arc has a scale spanning 30° and is graduated in degrees. On the upper arc there is a sliding vane with a

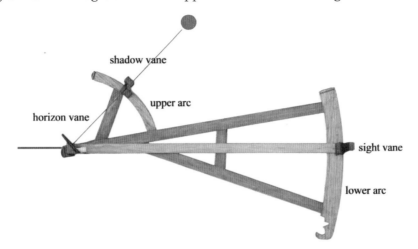

shadow vane

upper arc

horizon vane

sight vane

lower arc

pinhole through which the sun's light passes. This is known as the shadow vane because it was originally used to cast a shadow rather than a pinpoint of light. At the fore end of the staff there's a slotted vane on which the pinhole of sunlight falls. This is called the horizon vane because the horizon is viewed through the slot. Finally, a sliding vane containing a pinhole or eyepiece is mounted on the lower arc. This is called the sight vane.

How to make the back-staff

The following materials will make a back-staff 53cm (21in) long and 31cm (12in) high.

- **Frame and sliding vanes**
  hardwood 2300mm (8ft) × 21mm × 15mm

- **Index arm**
  hardwood 530mm × 21mm × 4mm

- **Horizon vane**
  hardwood 90mm × 45mm × 4mm

- A nut, bolt and washers

- Copies of the lower arc scale and vernier scale (Appendix 3)

- Transparent adhesive film

- Adhesive and screws

- Spirit level (optional)

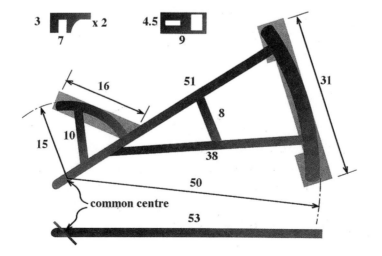

1. The drawing shows the general layout of the back-staff with the approximate length of each section. Note the common centre which plays an important part in the design and operation. Join the various parts with wood glue and screws.

2. The upper and lower arcs are made by scarfing two or more pieces of wood and cutting them to shape as shown in the drawing. Glue and pin them to the frame but leave their outer edges unfinished at this stage.

3. Cut out the index arm and attach it to the frame through the common centre with a nut and bolt. Using the arm and a pencil as compasses, mark the circumference of the two arcs and sand them carefully to shape.

4. Cut a small slot (30mm × 5mm) in the horizon vane. The vane will be stronger and look better if it encloses the staff and a suitable aperture should be provided. Attach the vane to the index bar at about 45° and supported by a small block of wood then draw a line across the vane from the common centre to the slot.

5. The shadow and sight vanes are made as shown in the drawing and photographs. Note the small post on the top of the sight vane; this will hold the vernier scale. Sand the inside of both vanes so they match the curve of the arc on which they sit. To help them slide smoothly, line them with a layer of sail repair tape. The pinholes may be drilled with a fine drill or a hot darning needle. If the line of the pinhole is inaccurate, drill a larger hole, pack it with filler, and start again. When the shadow vane is placed anywhere on the upper arc, its pinhole should point directly to a point on the line between the common centre and the slot in the horizon vane. Mark this point clearly with a dot. Glue the sight vane to the index arm.

Preparing the scales

Although the original versions had their scales on the sides of the arcs, on this version, the scales are mounted on the rims of the arcs. A copy of the back-staff's scale is presented in Appendix 3. Measure the distance between the common centre and the outer edge of the lower arc, multiply it by 3.1416 and divide the result by 6. This is the required length of the lower (30°) scale and can be obtained by using the enlarging and reducing facilities of a copying machine. Include the small vernier scale when adjusting and copying the lower scale.

The vernier scale

The principle of the vernier scale is described in most encyclopedias and an example of how it works is shown below. The lower scale for this back-staff is graduated in 10' divisions and the vernier scale is used to determine the precise position occupied by the zero within one of these divisions. In the example, the zero is just past 19°20' and the vernier coincides with the main scale at 4. The reading on the lower arc is therefore 19°20' + 4' = 19°24'.

Glue the vernier scale to the small post at the side of the sight vane. Clamp the index arm in line with the central staff. Then attach the 30° scale to the rim of the lower arc, making sure that 0° coincides with the zero on the vernier scale. Protect the surface of scale with transparent adhesive film.

The upper scale

Use a protractor at the common centre to establish positions on the upper arc at 10° intervals. Place the pinhole of the shadow vane in line with these positions and mark the rim of the arc using the front edge of the vane as a guide. These upper scale graduations are a temporary measure, and will need adjusting following field trials with known altitudes. Once you've established the most accurate positions, you may find a suitable way of locking the shadow vane on these settings.

Added refinements

Why not add an artificial horizon? Drill a hole into the horizon vane and its wooden support large enough to house the end of a small spirit level. Lightly clamp the index arm and line up the vanes on the horizon. In the absence of a real horizon, use a long spirit level or the two water levels in a U-shaped length of winemaker's hose. When the index bar is horizontal, adjust and glue the small spirit level so the bubble is in its central position. A small improvement may be made to the dot or target on the horizon vane by inserting the head of a pin and painting a small white disc around it. When the sunlight hits the target correctly the head of the pin will sparkle.

Using the back-staff

Stand with your back to the sun. Set the shadow vane on the upper arc to the nearest 10° below the sun's altitude. View the horizon through the sight and the horizon vanes and gradually move the sight vane down the lower arc until the pinhole of sunlight hits the target and lines up with the horizon. The observed altitude is the combined measurement of both arcs. To use the artificial horizon, hold the back-staff in front of you with the sun on your right. Adjust the sight vane until the pinhole of sunlight shines on the pin head with the bubble in the centre of the spirit level.

You can verify the consistency of the scales by comparing different vane settings on the same altitude. For example, if the meridian altitude is 62°30' (60° + 2°30') check to see if an upper scale setting of 50° is accompanied by a lower scale setting of 12°30', or a 40° setting by 22°30'. Although the device can measure to within 1' of arc, don't anticipate this level of accuracy in practice. If your meridian altitude places you within 5' of true latitude, you can be well pleased with your efforts.

Henry the octant

The octant was invented by John Hadley in 1731 and there are several examples on view in the National Maritime Museum at Greenwich.

The octant was the forerunner to the sextant and is capable of measuring angles up to 90°, whereas a sextant can measure angles up to 120°. In an octant or a sextant, the image of a celestial object is brought in line with the horizon through two mirrors and remains steady on the horizon as long as the angle between the two mirrors is not altered. The octant soon replaced the back-staff as the ideal solution for shipboard observations. This octant cost about £2 ($3) to make from junk and answers to the name of Henry after the famous Portuguese navigator.

How to make the octant

Materials

- Hardwood 1250mm × 15mm × 21mm
- Nut, bolt and washers
- Lens from cheap plastic binoculars
- Layers of dark 35mm film
- A thin mirror
- Brass sheeting (for embellishment)
- Scale and vernier (Appendix 3)
- Drawer handle
- Adhesive and varnish

The octant's frame is made from pieces of hardwood (15mm × 21mm) glued and screwed together. Curved sections, such as the main arc, are made by scarfing several pieces together, cutting and sanding them to shape. The moving index arm is also made from wood, and pivots smoothly around an adjustable nut and bolt through a point near the top of the frame. The overall dimensions of the frame are: height 310mm and width 230mm (12in × 9in).

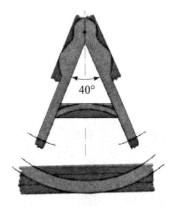

The mirrors, known as the index and horizon glasses, were cut from a discarded powder compact, glued to wooden supports, then firmly attached to the index arm and the main frame respectively. The back surface of the index glass must line up with the pivot point. The horizon glass is only half a mirror and allows the observer to see the object's reflection and look at the

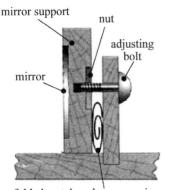

mirror support
nut
adjusting bolt
mirror
folded metal wedge as a spring

horizon at the same time. Place some tape halfway across the back of the mirror and gently rub off the reflecting material with a light abrasive cleaner until half of the mirror is clear. Its position is a matter of trial and error depending on the location of the telescope. Both glasses need a means of adjustment to keep them perpendicular to the plane of the instrument and this is provided by a post and an adjusting screw behind each support. To maintain pressure on the adjusting screw, a thin strip of brass sheeting is folded over and wedged between the post and the mirror support as shown here. It's a crude arrangement but very effective.

Earlier octants were provided with a simple sighting aid, but a telescope improves the instrument's accuracy. This one was made from a short piece of bamboo with lenses from a pair of plastic binoculars and attached to the frame by a dowel. The index glass shade was made using the dark ends of a 35mm black-and-white negative film; three layers are adequate in

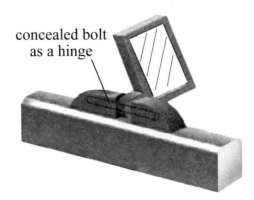

concealed bolt as a hinge

reducing the glare of the sun.
The shade is attached to the
frame of the octant as shown
here. Two parallel shades, one
weak and one strong, would be
more effective in coping with
different levels of brightness.
Note. When observing the sun
and its reflection through an

artificial horizon, it's essential to have a similar shading arrangement
on the horizon glass or a shaded eyepiece on the telescope.

The scale

On Henry, the 90° scale is mounted underneath the arc and its length
is related to the distance between the pivot point and the arc by the
following formula:

length of 90° scale = (distance $\times$ 3.1416)/4

Copy the octant's scale from Appendix 3. and enlarge it according
to the formula. The scale can be checked by working out different

altitudes from a known position. If you
are landlocked then the use of an artificial
horizon is invaluable. This involves
measuring and halving the angle between
an object and its reflection in a bowl of oil
or water, and is very handy for verifying
the upper end of the scale.

The foot of the index arm contains a
vernier scale which allows

closer readings than are possible with the main
scale alone. The main scale is graduated in
20' divisions and the vernier scale is used
to determine the precise position occupied
by the zero within one of these divisions.

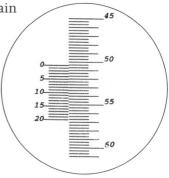

In the example here, the zero is just past
50°20' and the vernier coincides with
the scale at 8'. The reading, therefore, is

$50°20' + 8' = 50°28'$. Fine adjustments to the readings can be made with a tangent screw – a thin brass bolt which is clamped to the arc and moves the index arm forwards and backwards. It is not absolutely necessary and the arm can be set quite accurately by gentle nudging. I think Captain Cook managed without a tangent screw so if you omit this feature you are in good company. The handle is from a drawer, and the frame is finished in woodstain, burnished with rubbing compound, and embellished with strips of flexible brass sheeting from a model shop.

The octant in use

Prior to use, the index and horizon mirrors must be checked and adjusted to ensure they are perpendicular to the plane of the instrument.

First adjustment. The index mirror is perpendicular when the main arc and its reflection coincide when viewed obliquely from the top of the instrument.

Second adjustment. The horizon glass is perpendicular when a distant object, such as a star, and its reflection appear in a vertical line. The index arm should be set close to zero.

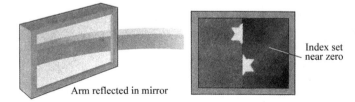

Arm reflected in mirror

Index set near zero

The mirrors are parallel when the star and its reflection appear as one and the index arm is set at $0°$. As no adjustment is provided here, the scale has to be positioned initially and checked regularly by this method; any subsequent error is applied to the reading. This is the instrument's index error.

Other adjustments to the octant's reading include refraction and height of eye. The closer the object to the horizon, the more it is affected by atmospheric refraction which makes it appear higher than it is. Similarly, the altitude increases with the height of the observer above sea level. Both of these corrections must be deducted from the observed altitude. For example, at an observed altitude of $5°$ the error is $10'$, at 10° it is about 5', and at 20° about 2.5'. At a height of eye of 3 metres (10 ft), the correction is about 3' and at a height of 12 metres it is about 6'.

Armed with a nautical almanac, tables, watch and calculator, I've taken numerous sights with Henry using the horizon at sea, or an artificial horizon. After standard adjustments, the readings are usually within 1.5' of the true altitude. In practical terms this means a position within one or two miles of the correct one.

The basic principles of a sextant

1. Octants and sextants share the same basic principle. When an object is reflected by two mirrors which are in the same plane, the angle between the object and its final image is double the angle between the two mirrors.

2. If the mirrors are adjusted so the image appears to coincide with the observer's horizon, then the object's height above the horizon will be double the angle between the two mirrors.

3. The angle between the mirrors is controlled and measured by an arm which swings over a graduated scale. The scale provides the correct reading by doubling the angle between the mirrors. This explains why a sextant's scale measures angles up to 120° but only extends over 60° – one sixth of a circle, whence originates the name sextant.

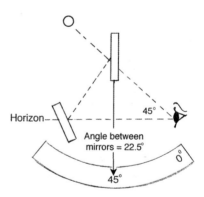

4. A double-reflected image of an object remains stable regardless of any vertical movement affecting both mirrors, e.g. rocking the device. This is why a sextant is ideal for observing altitudes at sea.

Dire straits navigation

Dire straits navigation is an emergency method of navigation. It is remarkably simple and only requires a watch set to GMT and a few everyday objects. Experience has shown that it is capable of providing a calculated position within several miles of the true one. Not perfect, but good enough if you are lost in the middle of the Pacific. To follow the instructions below, you should have a basic understanding of latitude and longitude, the Greenwich meridian, the dates of the solstices (21 June, 21 December), the equinoxes (21 March, 23 September – the odd one out), and the number of days in each month.

Requirements

- A watch set to GMT

- A square sheet of paper (approx 20cm × 20cm)

- A wooden board (the back of a locker?)

- A few panel pins

- A ruler (useful but not essential)

- A poem

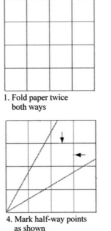

1. Fold paper twice both ways

2. Fold corner to centreline

2. Fold opposite corner to centreline

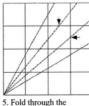

4. Mark half-way points as shown

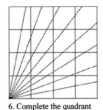

5. Fold through the two points

6. Complete the quadrant using the 3 middle sectors

First you will construct a simple quadrant with the paper and the wooden board. Then you will need to know the sun's position in relation to the equator (its declination) and the time at which it passes the Greenwich meridian on the day of the observation. Assuming you do not have an almanac, these data can be calculated with the help of four letters of the alphabet and a poem.

Stage 1. To construct the quadrant

Fold your sheet of paper as shown in the diagram. This will give you a protractor with nine 10° sectors. A ruler may be used to mark up the individual degrees within a particular 10° sector.

Paste the paper quadrant on a board and tap in some panel pins along the horizon line as shown below – two sighting pins and one horizon pin. Viewed from the sighting pins, the horizon pin will blink when the sun's shadow from the shadow pin falls across it. Instructions on how to set the shadow pin follow later.

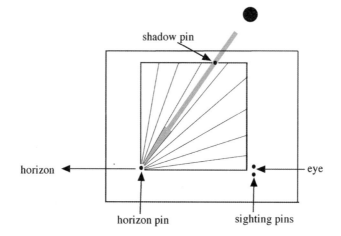

Stage 2. To calculate the sun's declination

The sun crosses the equator northwards around 21 March and southwards around 23 September each year and reaches its maximum declination of 23.45° north or south roughly 92 days later. Note the convenient sequence of numbers in the sun's maximum declination.

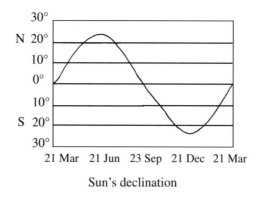

Sun's declination

The key figures to remember are 8, 15, 20 and 23. Converting these numbers to letters of the alphabet and placing them in a sentence such as 'Help On The Way' may work as a memory jogger. These are the latitudes the sun will have reached each 20 days it is from the equator. So it takes

the first 20 days to reach a declination of 8°
the next 20 days to reach a declination of 15°
the next 20 days to reach a declination of 20°
the next 20 days to reach a declination of 23°
the remaining days to reach a declination of 23.45°

With a diary and some simple arithmetic, you should be able to work out the sun's declination to within half a degree or closer. For example, 14 April is 24 days after 21 March. This is 4 days or one fifth of the next 20 days in the table. One fifth between 8° and 15° is about 9.4°. The declination on 14 April, therefore, is about 9.4° and is north. Note that over a four-year period there are annual variations in the sun's daily declination. For the level of accuracy required here, these can be ignored, but during a leap year (after 28 February) it is worth calculating the figure for the day following the one in which the observations are being made.

Stage 3. To calculate the time at which the sun transits Greenwich

The time at which the sun crosses the Greenwich meridian varies from about 1144 to 1214 GMT throughout the year. This is due to a tilt in the earth's axis and its elliptical motion around the sun. Although this variation or 'equation of time' changes very gradually, it follows a fairly complex pattern as can be seen from the graph on the right.

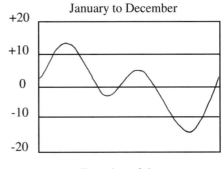

January to December

Equation of time

In the absence of an almanac or diagram, it is possible to calculate the time of the Greenwich transit with the help of the following rhyme inspired by David Burch's excellent book, *Emergency Navigation.*

14 minutes late around Valentine's day
 4 minutes early in the middle of May
 6 minutes late near the end of July
16 minutes early when halloween's nigh
      The figures last about two weeks
      either side of these four peaks

The last two lines are a reminder that the variations last about two weeks either side of the dates listed before they start to change. With a diary and some simple arithmetic, the equation of time may be calculated for specific days to within a minute of the correct figure. For example, to find the equation of time for 9 April, calculate the period from two weeks after Valentine's day to two weeks before the middle of May, i.e. about 61 days. 9 April is 40 days into this period, i.e. about two thirds of 61 days. Two thirds of the 18 minutes range (+14 minutes to −4 minutes) is about 12 minutes. So the equation of time is 14 − 12 minutes = 2 minutes. On 9 April, the sun crosses the Greenwich meridian at approximately 1202hrs.

Stage 4. To find latitude

Using trial and error, tap in a shadow pin close to where you think the sun's altitude will be at local noon. With your back to the sun, aim the device at the horizon. Look along the sighting pins to the horizon pin, rock the device up and down and see if the horizon pin blinks. If it blinks below the horizon, the shadow pin is to low. If it blinks above the horizon, the pin is too high. When you have got it right, read the sun's altitude from the scale and deduct it from 90°. The result is the angle between your zenith and the sun (below). In navigation, this angle is known as the zenith distance.

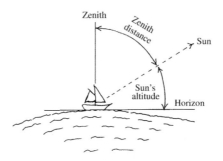

Zenith distance = 90° - sun's altitude

To calculate latitude, think where the sun lies in relation to you and the equator.

- If the sun is between you and the equator, add the sun's declination to the zenith distance.

- If the equator is between you and the sun, deduct the sun's declination from the zenith distance.

For example, at noon on a particular day, the sun has a declination of 11.5° north. The sun's altitude is found to be 61° so its zenith distance is 29°. The sun lies between the observer and the equator, so the declination is added to the zenith distance. The latitude, therefore, is 29° + 11.5° = 40.5° north. If you have got this far, you might like to work out the appropriate formula when the observer's position lies between the sun and the equator.

Stage 5. To find longitude

The earth rotates 15° each hour (1° every 4 minutes; 0.25° every minute). The difference in time between the sun's transit over the Greenwich meridian and its transit over the observer's meridian can be converted directly to a longitude. For example, a time difference of 3 hours 12 minutes before Greenwich converts to a longitude of 48° east of Greenwich. A time difference of 11 hours 10 minutes after Greenwich converts to a longitude of 167.5° west of Greenwich.

This is how to time the sun's transit over your meridian. A couple of hours before local noon, tap in a shadow pin on the edge of the scale, aim the device at the horizon and time when the horizon pin blinks. Do not remove the pin. When the sun has descended to the same height after noon, note the time of the second set of observation. The sun's transit over the meridian will have taken place midway between these observations. It is advisable to take several before and after observations, rather than rely on a single pair of observations, and average the results. It also assumes that your position has remained unchanged in the intervening period.

For example, on 6 February, the estimated times of the sun's transit over the meridian averaged 1555 GMT. The transit at Greenwich was 1214 GMT. This difference of 3 hours 41 minutes after Greenwich indicated a longitude of 55.25° (55°15') west.

Finally, here are a couple of alternatives to the shadow pin quadrant.

An emergency quadrant

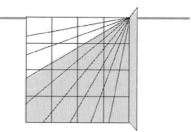

An emergency quadrant can be made by using a rectangular sheet of stiff paper. After the protractor has been constructed as described earlier, fold the unused portion at a right angle to the scale. The device is then held upright at 90° to the sun and aligned with the horizon as shown in the diagram. It's a good idea to keep it out of the wind if you can.

An emergency sextant

Partly open the lid of an audio cassette holder. With the opening at the top, and your eyes protected from the sun ahead, look through the container and a reflected image of the sun will appear. Adjust the angle

of the open lid until the sun's image appears to coincide with the horizon. If the lid is made secure, the image will remain stable as when using a sextant. Use this device to take and time morning and afternoon observations of the sun. The mean of these times is when the sun is over your meridian.

The moon as your compass

How can you tell the direction of north or south
from a waxing or waning moon?

As the moon will be either east or west of the
sun, the line separating the light and dark surfaces
of the moon will be aligned roughly in a north
and south.direction.

Survive!

You are sailing in the yacht *Sea Slug* in a shipping lane midway between
Panama and New Zealand. Unfortunately, someone left the chip pan
burning in the galley. *Sea Slug* caught fire and is about to sink. You send
a distress signal and scramble into the lifeboat. Here are some items
you could take with you. Rank them 1 to 15 according to their
importance for your survival.

Mosquito net	Sail	Water
Shark repellent	Length of rope	Survival rations
Spare oar	Portable radio	Knife
Paraffin	Compass	Compact mirror
Pacific Ocean chart	Matches	Fishing kit

Make your own choice first and then share your ideas with others
before looking at the notes on page 146.

Killorain's treasure island

There is supposed to be treasure buried on Pinaki atoll, but so far no one has found it.

A 1940s British Government guide to the Pacific Islands

In 1958, whilst working on the 10-knot trampship mentioned earlier, I passed near Pinaki and was intrigued by the thought of treasure buried on this lonely atoll. Over the years, I have researched the story of the treasure and this is what I have discovered. Perhaps we may meet up one day with the same purpose in mind but it won't be on Pinaki atoll.

In 1912, Charles Edward Howe, a Cornishman living in Australia, was disturbed one stormy evening by the sound of someone outside his front door. He looked out and saw an old tramp sheltering from the rain. Howe took pity on the man, who was Irish, and gave him a meal and some dry clothes. When the storm had abated, he took him to the nearest bus station and gave him the fare to Sydney. Several weeks later, he received a message from a hospital asking him to visit a patient who was dying. Puzzled, he went to the hospital where he discovered that the dying man was none other than the tramp he had briefly befriended. Lying in the darkness of a deserted ward, the old fellow summoned the strength to tell him an astonishing tale: a tale which led Howe, and may even lead you, to an atoll in the South Seas in search of buried treasure.

The man said his name was Joseph Killorain and that he was born in 1825 in County Clare. In 1858 he deserted a sailing ship along with three unsavoury colleagues: Diego Alvarez, a Spaniard, Archer Brown, an Australian, and Luke Barret, an American. They made their way to Pisco, a seaport on the coast of Peru, where they had heard of a church with a huge quantity of gold concealed in its vaults. The four worked around the harbour and became regular worshippers at mass. Having won the trust of the local priest, they told him that they had overheard a conversation in a bar between two thieves who were planning to rob the church. Why, Joseph had even heard one of thieves mentioned by name! The parish priest recognised it as that of a young curate who had served in the church some years earlier but who had deserted the priesthood for a woman. This convinced him that evil deeds were afoot and he sought the four men's help in transferring the gold to another church further up the coast. They solemnly swore not to tell another soul and they had every intention of keeping that promise! The gang made its move when the gold was safely aboard a small sailing ship, the *Bosun Bird*, in transit to Callao. They overpowered the other members of the crew and threw them overboard. Then, having disposed of the the two priests who were guarding the gold, they fled westwards into the Pacific Ocean.

In December 1859, the *Bosun Bird* anchored in the harbour at Tahiti to take on fresh water and provisions. The port records show that officials did not board her as she carried a signal indicating there was fever aboard. From Tahiti, she sailed east to the Tuamotus, an area of several hundred small atolls and reefs. Many of these small islands were unchartered and most were deserted. Killorain and the gang decided to bury their ill-gotten gains on a deserted island and return later when any hue and cry had died down. Having found a suitable island, they buried some gold on the beach close to a large column of coral which overlooked the entrance to the lagoon. Then they dropped the rest of the gold into a pear-shaped pool to the side of the lagoon. Crossing to a distant island, they asked a native the name of the island they had visited. He told them that it sounded like Pinaki or an island near it. Later, Alvarez killed this man, a brutal act which Killorain deeply regretted. Leaving the Tuamotus, they followed the trade winds to Australia and scuttled the *Bosun Bird* on a reef near Cooktown. The quartet rowed ashore to begin new lives in preparation for their return to the island, but here their luck ran out. By February 1860, two had been killed in a fight, and two were in jail for manslaughter following a brawl in a bar. Brown died before completing his sentence and Joseph Killorain was the sole survivor. He never returned to the Tuamotus but, after many years in prison, drifted penniless around Australia and New Zealand. Killorain thanked Howe for the kindness he had shown him earlier and handed over a greasy piece of cloth which contained an outline of the island and the whereabouts of the treasure. After Howe left, Killorain received the last rites from a priest and died some hours later.

At first, Howe was very doubtful about the whole tale, but he checked up on Killorain's story and found much of it to be true. Having no family ties, he sold his property and set off to search Pinaki, which he reached in February 1913. According to the map some of

the booty was buried 84 feet east, and some 75 feet north, of a tall
column of coral. Pinaki, however, contained several such columns, so
Howe dug a complex network of trenches along the lagoon beach.
He didn't find a thing. There were many times when he cursed the
Irishman who had led him on what seemed to be a wild goose chase,
but he stuck to his task. In 1919, the writer Charles Nordhoff (Mutiny
on the Bounty) was becalmed off Pinaki in the schooner Potii Ravarava
and, on going ashore, was astonished to discover Howe furiously
digging up the beach. He spent three days with Howe, who told him
much of this tale.

Howe abandoned his search and returned to Tahiti after nearly
14 years. Only then did he discover that some Polynesians pronounce
their t's almost like p's. Could the four pirates have misheard Pinaki
instead of Tinaki? Howe studied charts of the area and found a small
island with a name similar to that. He visited the atoll and eventually
discovered one nearby that contained the key features of the treasure
map. It is my belief that he explored islands in the vicinity of
Tuanake atoll.

Back in Tahiti, Howe had a disagreement with some government
officials and was deported from the Tuamotus. Returning to Australia,
he made contact with a group of investors and told them that he had
located the site of the treasure. He offered to share it with them if they
would finance a well-equipped search. Then, just before the expedition
left Australia, he went to visit some friends in the outback, fell ill and
died. As his backers had been entrusted with the map, they decided to
go ahead and sailed from Tahiti on 25 February 1934 on the schooner
Guisborne. But they were ill-prepared for conditions on the atoll and
suffered badly from heat stroke and coral fever. Discouraged, and dogged
by financial setbacks, the group abandoned the project and returned
home empty-handed. Later, one of the team wrote an account of the
expedition with numerous photographs but did not reveal the island's
identity. The years passed and the search for the Pisco gold was forgotten.

The story of the Pisco gold has always intrigued me since passing
Pinaki atoll as a boy on the way to New Zealand. With the help of the
Bishop Museum in Tahiti, I obtained aerial photographs and maps of
the atolls in that region. One atoll in this labyrinth of coral islands and
reefs looks much like any other, and information about the smaller
atolls is often inaccurate or misleading. I studied them for many hours
and then one evening found myself staring down at a photo of

Killorain's treasure island. There, on the edge of the lagoon, was the pear-shaped pool shimmering in the sun, and guarding the beach at the entrance to the lagoon stood a large column of coral. The surveyors had used the column of coral as a triangulation point and recorded its exact position. It is 16°49' south and 144°16' west of Greenwich. So now you have it! Perhaps you are inspired to continue the search. It will be a supreme challenge of your sailing, navigation and pilotage skills. And we both know that you will not be heading for Pinaki.

A few words of advice to would-be treasure hunters. You can sail to the atoll from Tahiti in less than two days, but the waters surrounding the Tuamotus are considered to be among the most difficult and dangerous in the world. Seven-knot currents often sweep the unwary mariner directly across the reefs. Avoid the hurricane season months of November to March. Landing on a reef, even in the lee of the atoll, can be tricky but the pass into the lagoon is deep enough for a small yacht. Or, leave your yacht in Tahiti and hitch a lift to the atoll on a passing copra boat if you don't mind rain-soaked clothing,

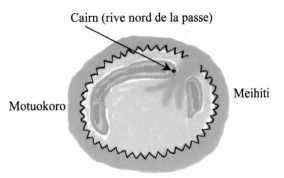

Cairn (rive nord de la passe)

Motuokoro

Meihiti

seasickness, diesel fumes, and enormous cockroaches. I advise you to take a good metal detector, underwater diving equipment, a sharp knife, and a pick and shovel. You will also need drinking water, shark repellent, and a large first aid kit. Watch out for rats and take the time to read up about moray eels. These water snakes with large teeth are often found lurking in pools by the reef. I wish you well, but don't blame me if you encounter the bad luck that seems to have dogged earlier searches. On the other hand, you could buy Admiralty chart no. 998 of the Tuamotu Archipelago, hang it in your den, and dream.

A seafarer's sundial

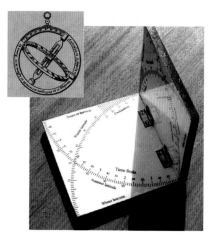

This device is based on the universal ring dial, a 17th-century invention which served both as a compass and as a clock. It was popular with navigators because neither function was dependent on a knowledge of the other. Redesigned, it is presented here as an emergency navigation aid which, when used in conjunction with the sun, GMT and the tables provided, will provide a rough estimate of one's latitude and longitude and an accurate direction of north or south. With practice it's easy to use, but it's quite a challenge to describe so follow the examples carefully using the figures mentioned in the text.

Constructing the dial

Make an enlarged copy of the scale below and paste it onto a firm base with the two halves exactly at right angles to each other. This can be a permanent arrangement like a book-end, or it can be hinged for easy storage (see photo). Make sure that the upper and lower edges of the base are aligned accurately with the scale. Protect the scale with some adhesive transparent film.

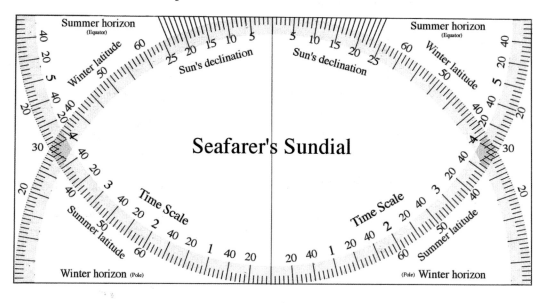

Using the dial to find north or south and longitude

On one face of the dial, you place a marker on the sun's declination
and draw a line representing your latitude. When the dial is correctly
aligned with the horizon, the sun casts a jagged shadow on the other
face. When this shadow touches the time scale, the dial is pointing
exactly north or south. The time scale indicates the hours and minutes
before (or after) the sun's passage over your meridian and this figure
is used to calculate your longitude.

Here are two examples of how the dial works. In both cases, the
latitude is estimated to be 38° north and the sun is ascending. In the
first example, the sun's declination is 10° north (summer) and in the
second example it is 10° south (winter).

Summer observation (observer faces the equator)

1. On the left-hand face of the dial, place a
    marker on the declination scale at 10° and
    draw a line to 38° on the summer latitude
    scale. The marker can be a small piece of
    card pinned or glued to the scale.

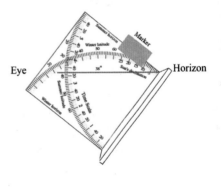

2. Face in the direction of the equator.

3. Align the upper edge of the other face
    with the horizon and rotate the device up
    or down until the latitude line you have
    drawn also appears to be in line with the
    horizon.

4. Hold this alignment and swing left or
    right until the jagged shadow cast by the
    marker crosses the time scale.

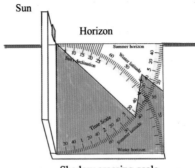

5. You are now facing exactly south and
    the time scale shows the hours and
    minutes before the sun crosses your
    meridian. This will be converted to
    longitude as explained later.

Shadow crossing scale
at 3 hrs and 12 mins

Winter observation (observer faces the nearest pole)

1. On the right-hand face of the dial, place a marker on the declination scale at 10° and draw a line to 38° on the winter latitude scale.

2. Face the nearest pole.

3. Align the lower edge of the other face with the horizon and rotate the dial up or down until the latitude line you have drawn also appears to be in line with the horizon.

3. Hold this alignment and swing left or right until the jagged shadow cast by the marker crosses the time scale.

4. You are now facing exactly north and the time scale shows the hours and minutes before the sun crosses your meridian.

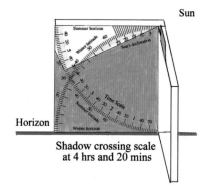

Shadow crossing scale
at 4 hrs and 20 mins

For afternoon observations, the dial's faces would switch roles and the time scale would indicate the hours and minutes after local transit.

Converting the time scale to longitude

With the sun ascending, an observation was made at 1012 hrs GMT on 16 February and the sun's shadow crossed the time scale at 4 hours and 20 minutes.

	h	m	
Observation taken	10	12	GMT
Time scale (add)	4	20	
Meridian passage	14	32	GMT
Meridian passage at Greenwich (from tables)	12	14	GMT
Difference	2	18	after Greenwich

1 hour = 15° longitude, so 2 hours 18 minutes converts to 34.5°.
The transit occurred after Greenwich, so the observer must be west of
Greenwich and the longitude is approximately 34.5° west.

To find latitude

At noon, face 90° to the sun, hold the dial upright and align the upper
edge with the horizon. The protruding face will cast a shadow equal to
the sun's altitude on the other face. Read the altitude using the
summer latitude scale.

Remember that 90° − sun's altitude = zenith distance (ZX)

Sun is between observer and equator: ZX + declination = latitude
Equator is between observer and sun: ZX − declination = latitude
Observer is between the equator and sun: declination − ZX = latitude

Almanac data and measurements

Mount the table in Appendix 2 on the back of the dial. With careful
interpolation, you should get an estimate of the time the sun transits
the Greenwich meridian to within half a minute, and its declination to
within a quarter of a degree, for any day of the year. Over a four-year
period there are annual variations in the sun's daily declination, but for
the level of accuracy here these may be ignored. After 28 February in
a leap year, it is worth calculating the figure for the day following the
one in which the observation is made. As with all simple horizon-
aligned devices, you have to be very patient and persevere in your
measurements. Better results are obtained when the sun is a couple of
hours or more from the meridian and the average of a series of
observations will usually be more accurate than relying on a single
observation.

Latitude and longitude by compass

Although the sun is often used to check compass accuracy, the compass itself usually plays little part in position finding by astronavigation. Bearings by compass are usually too broad or unreliable for the accuracy required. There are, however, some occasions when the compass can help – particularly as a back-up or an emergency procedure. Two such approaches are described here and they may help to while away an idle hour on watch, or come in useful one day when the fat controllers switch off the satellites.

Longitude by compass (a)

In popular descriptions of astro-navigation, the measurement of longitude is often explained as the time difference between the sun's transit at Greenwich and its transit over the observer's meridian, a difference of four minutes of time representing 1° of longitude. In practice, timing the exact moment of the sun's transit over one's meridian (local apparent noon) is not easily achieved and longitude is established by more complex procedures. In emergency navigation, however, the simplicity of this approach makes it worth considering. It is particularly suitable where the sun is at a low altitude, or when it is partially obscured by cloud. A reasonable level of accuracy may be achieved if the compass error is known to within one degree. The compass needs a carefully adjusted prism or mirror to lower an image of the sun to the horizon or thereabouts, and some shades to cut out any glare.

The procedure involves taking and timing a number of bearings of the sun as it approaches, passes, and leaves the meridian. The more azimuths or bearings recorded, the more accurate the final result. These data are plotted on a graph with coordinates representing bearings and time. A line is drawn which best fits the plotted data, and, with the help of the known compass error, this is used to determine the time of the meridian transit.

Here is a worked example off the west coast of Ireland. A magnetic handbearing compass was used with a known error of 7.5° west. This meant that the compass card would overestimate the true bearing by 7.5°, i.e. the sun would be on the meridian when bearing 187.5°.

February 2001   Compass Error 7.5° West

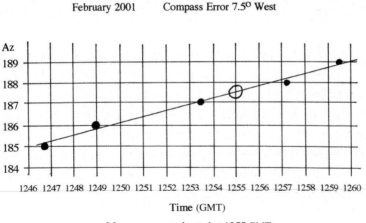

Time (GMT)

Mean passage estimated at 1255 GMT

From the graph above, the estimated time of the sun's transit was 1255 GMT. On 6 February 2001, the transit at Greenwich was 1214 GMT. This difference of 41 minutes after Greenwich indicated a longitude of 10°15' west. The correct longitude was 10°10' west, but this is emergency navigation not GPS. Had there been some doubt over the compass error, the graph could have been used to find a range of longitude. Even if only a couple of observations are obtained one side or the other of noon, it is still possible to prepare a simple graph and extend the line to estimate the time of local noon.

Longitude by compass (b)

The sun's LHA is the difference between the sun's longitude and the observer's longitude. Imagine how easy it would be to calculate longitude if you could read the sun's LHA with the help of a compass. It may sound far-fetched but it can be done – though there is a catch. The bearing has to be taken when the sun's altitude is the same as its declination. Also, the bearing is reported with reference to the quadrant in which it lies. For example, a bearing of 160° = S20°E. and a bearing of 310° = N50°W. With this simple conversion, you have the LHA. It's as easy as that and it even works when the observer's latitude and sun's declination are in different hemispheres. The procedure requires a watch set to GMT, a sun quadrant, and a suitable compass with a known error. A sextant (adjusted to compensate for the sun's semi-diameter and refraction) will provide a more accurate observation but much will depend on the accuracy of the compass reading. Here is an example near the island of Martinique when the sun was descending in the west.

Date:	1 November
Sun's declination:	14°30' S
Altitude required:	14°30'
Observation timed at:	2028 GMT
Sun's bearing:	250.5° or S70.5°W
Sun's GHA @ 2028 on 1 November:	131.1°
Sun's LHA (see converted bearing):	070.5°
GHA − LHA = observer's longitude:	060.6° west

If an almanac is unavailable, the sun's GHA may be obtained by calculating the difference between the time of the observation and the sun's transit at Greenwich. On 1 November, the sun transits Greenwich at about 1144hrs. 20h28m − 11h44m = 08h44m. At a rate of 15° per hour, 08h44m = 131°.

To be frank, as a means of finding longitude, this method usually leaves something to be desired and the word accuracy springs to mind. But give it a try sometime: it may surprise you.

Latitude by compass

This unusual way of finding one's latitude by compass requires so little effort and information that it may seem unbelievable, but it works – particularly at higher latitudes. It does not require an almanac, GMT, or even an accurate compass reading. It demands, however, precise measurements with a sextant and an efficient timekeeper, and is limited to the summer months of either hemisphere.

Basic principle

If the sun's declination is the same sign but smaller than your latitude, it will pass to the east or west. When it is bearing almost due east or west, the rate or speed at which it ascends or descends is related to your latitude. For example, throughout the summer months in latitude 50° N, the sun will climb through east or descend through west at a rate of 9.65' per minute of time. In latitude 40° N, the rate increases to 11.5' and in latitude 30° it is about 13'. If you are able to measure the rate per minute at which the sun is rising or ascending the prime vertical, and measure it very accurately, then you can calculate your latitude.

Procedure

Take and time two readings of the sun's altitude when it is roughly bearing east (085° to 095°) or west (265° to 275°). You could try to capture the sun either side of east or west, but this is not essential and it is more important to keep within the compass bearings above. The longer the period between the two observations, the more accurate will be the result. If you wish, you can average out several before and after observations.

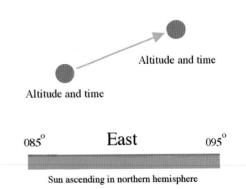

Next work out the change in the sun's altitude per minute. For example, if two observations were taken exactly 20 minutes apart and the change of altitude between observations was 3°45' (225'), the rate per minute would be 225/20 = 11.25'. To convert this to a latitude, you can use the table below or the formula on the next page.

Sun's change of altitude per minute on the Prime Vertical

Rate	Lat	Rate	Lat	Rate	Lat
7.5	60	10.8	44	13.12	29
7.73	59	10.97	43	13.24	28
7.95	58	11.15	42	13.36	27
8.17	57	11.32	41	13.48	26
8.39	56	11.49	40	13.60	25
8.60	55	11.66	39	13.70	24
8.81	54	11.82	38	13.81	23
9.03	53	11.98	37	13.90	22
9.23	52	12.14	36	14.00	21
9.44	51	12.29	35	14.10	20
9.64	50	12.44	34	------------	
9.84	49	12.58	33	14.49	15
10.03	48	12.72	32	14.77	10
10.23	47	12.86	31	14.94	5
10.42	46	12.99	30	15.00	0
10.60	45				

The formula

$$\frac{\text{Change of altitude per minute}}{15} = \text{Cosine of the latitude}$$

Using the table, a rate per minute of 11.25' gives a latitude of about 41°25'.

Using the formula, 11.25 divided by 15 = 0.75 which is the cosine of 41.4° = a latitude of 41°24'.

Latitude by compass is a useful exercise for those who enjoy using a sextant and wish to challenge their sight-taking skills. Try it out afloat with a real horizon or ashore with an artificial one. Use it in combination with the longitude finding method outlined in 'Sun navigation in a nutshell' (pages 71–77). Don't anticipate unerring accuracy with the procedure and avoid taking sights when the sun is close to the horizon unless you are prepared to adjust the obtained altitudes for refraction. Finally, the same procedure may be used with any star and you don't even have to identify it. The stars' apparent progress around the earth is a little faster than that of the sun so the denominator in the formula above becomes 15.04.

Where the sky is blue

The station master leaned out from the door of the ticket booth. 'The night train to New York will be here in a couple of minutes,' he announced to the three people standing on the platform.

The boy had waited impatiently for its arrival. It was good of his elderly relatives to see him off on his first trip to sea, but he was tired of making small talk and was anxious to be on his way. The train rounded the bend and pulled into the station. 'Now be sure to write from your first port of call,' reminded Aunty Bessie. 'And steer clear of them foreign girls,' she added, giving a knowing wink.

Uncle Fred, straight from the Miner's Tavern, grinned at him affectionately. 'Good Luck, sailor boy!' The boy embraced his aunt and then swung a heavy bag over his shoulder. As he turned to shake his uncle's hand, the old man whispered 'Here's some advice my pa gave me when I was leaving home. When winter's twilight troubles you, steer to where the sky is blue. You remember that and you'll be just fine.'

Aunty Bessie lifted an imaginary glass to her lips, 'Don't mind old Fred, he's had one or two.' The boy smiled, 'I won't forget it, sir, and I won't forget you both. You've been like a real ma and pa to me.' He jumped aboard and waved farewell through the grime of the carriage windows. As the train departed, he collapsed with relief on an empty seat. When winter's twilight troubles you, steer to where the sky is blue. Even without one or two, Uncle Jim could say some mighty strange things. The train gathered speed and hurtled through the night to New York.

Several years passed and the boy matured into a young man. Having passed his exams, he signed on as a navigator aboard a small American freighter bound for the Caribbean. She was a rust bucket held together by one hundred layers of paint and ready for the breakers. Somewhere in the Gulf of Mexico, she was caught by the tail of a typhoon. Many larger ships and their crews were lost. Swamped by mountainous seas, things looked bleak and the crew huddled together in the wheelhouse waiting for the final order. If they abandoned ship they knew they would probably abandon their lives.

In the midst of this mayhem, the young man recalled his uncle's profound advice. He walked out on to the bridge and in a wild fury screamed at the elements, 'When winter's twilight troubles you, steer to where the sky is blue!'

Mistaking his outburst for an order, the helmsman altered course in the direction of a small break in the clouds. The captain swung round swiftly to countermand the order but, as he did so, the wind began to ease. A dozen pairs of eyes stared at him anxiously. 'Yeah,' he said, 'Keep her on that heading.' Within an hour, the seas subsided, the skies cleared and the ship continued peacefully on its voyage.

Later that evening, the captain returned to the wheelhouse and eyed his young navigator with suspicion. 'Now what was all that about?' he asked.

'It's something my uncle told me,' replied the young man, feeling somewhat embarrassed by his behaviour.

'This uncle of yours, is he some kind of witch doctor?'

'No sir,' replied the young man, 'He's just a miner from Pittsburgh.'

The captain continued staring at his navigator then gestured toward the chart table. 'Well, you better get it down in the logbook. You never know when we might need it again.'

The years thundered by and the young man, now older and wiser, returned home. At the station, he heard that his uncle was dying and went straight to the hospital. Lying in the darkness of the ward, the old man awoke from a drugged sleep. He recognised his visitor and whispered, 'When winter's twilight troubles you...' His voice faltered and the younger man continued, 'Steer to where the sky is blue.'

Uncle Fred smiled, 'So you never forgot what my old pa taught me.'

'No sir,' replied his nephew, holding back a tear. 'It may even have saved my life.' For several minutes, he sat silently holding the old man's withered hand and then he spoke. 'I never forgot it, but I never understood it. What did your pa mean by it?'

The old man stared bleakly from his bed; his breathing was shallow and he was very tired. It had been a long life and now it was time to leave. He beckoned for his nephew to draw nearer until their faces were almost touching. 'The truth is...' he whispered. There was a long pause for breath. 'The truth is...' Yet another long pause. A trolley trundled noisily along the corridor and somewhere above the building a clock chimed the hour. The old man made a supreme effort, 'The truth is, boy, I never had a goddam clue.'

The longitude game

For many centuries, navigators have been using the height of Polaris, the Pole Star, as a guide to their latitude in the northern hemisphere. That the same star may also help to determine one's longitude may seem a strange claim but it is a true one. You may like to test out this unusual approach to navigation as a game which can involve all members of the crew. It requires an accurate time check and a few simple calculations. In the event of failure or loss of GPS, it could serve as a useful emergency navigation technique – so make a note of your best performer.

Among the bright stars that appear to circle Polaris is Kochab. By extending four fingers at arm's length from Polaris you should have little difficulty in identifying it.

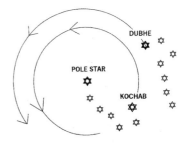

Although the Pole Star does not coincide exactly with the celestial pole, a line drawn from Polaris to Kochab passes almost directly through it. This means that when Kochab is directly above Polaris, it is almost exactly above your meridian of longitude. When the star lies 90° east or west of Polaris, it is almost 90° east or west of your longitude, and when it lies directly below Polaris, it is almost 180° from your longitude. 'Almost' means an error of about 0.25°. This small discrepancy, which varies only marginally with latitude, is removed in the calculations below.

Kochab is a circumpolar star about 16.5° from the Pole Star

The challenge is to judge when Kochab is at one of the four positions shown without the use of special instruments – and more about this later. Having timed the event by GMT, it is a relatively simple procedure to find the 'longitude' of Kochab with the help of an almanac and use it to calculate your own longitude. Although other circumpolar stars could be used, their errors are more complex and they are best avoided.

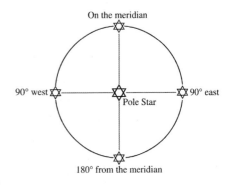

The alignment of Kochab and Polaris in relation to the observer's longitude.

Calculating the 'longitude' of Kochab

To avoid printing separate tables for each star, an almanac provides data for a single point in the heavens (Aries) and a table of additions for individual stars. For any given date and time, the tables show the distance (in degrees) that Aries is west of Greenwich. This is known as the Greenwich hour angle of Aries and is abbreviated to GHA Aries. By applying the addition for a particular star, the star's GHA is obtained. Although the GHA runs from 0° to 360°, it is easily converted to a longitude east or west of Greenwich. For example, a GHA of 245° is the same as a longitude of 115° east.

The procedure

1. From an almanac, or using Appendix 4, obtain the GHA of Aries at the time of the observation.

2. Add 137.55° for Kochab (this includes an adjustment for the discrepancy).

3. Add (or deduct) 0°, 90°, or 180° depending on the position of Kochab in relation to Polaris.

4 The result is your longitude east or west of Greenwich.

An example

On 5 June 2000, Kochab was observed to be directly above Polaris at 2352 GMT. The time was based on an average of crew member's observations. Our longitude, therefore, was approximately the same as Kochab's GHA.

GHA Aries at 2352 hrs	= 252.8°
Kochab's addition	= 137.55°
GHA Kochab	= 390.35°
Adjusted GHA Kochab	= 30.35° west
Longitude	= 30.35° or 30°21' west

The actual longitude was 30°15' west – not a perfect result but very acceptable for an emergency navigation technique.

Judging the position of Kochab

This is the challenging part. Some practice is needed to achieve this
with reasonable accuracy, and it is much easier with an unobstructed
view of the sky and some horizon visible. One approach is to focus on
Polaris until Kochab appears to be just before the required position
and note the time. Repeat the procedure when Kochab appears to be
just past the required position and take an average of the two times. As
a game, crew members can devise their own strategies for assessing
the alignment of Kochab with Polaris. For example, sighting along a
small plumb-line or spirit level will be of considerable help but only if
the yacht is fairly steady. Another approach is to line up the lower edge
of a book with the horizon and use the top or side edges to gauge the
stars' alignment. Ashore, with a plumb-line, the method can be
remarkably accurate. The winner is the member whose longitude is
closest to your known position.

Polarum

If you found the longitude game of interest, you may like to devise a Polarum. Whereas the game focused on four main positions of Kochab in relation to the Pole Star, Polarum can measure the angle of rotation at any time. This means that the technique of finding one's longitude can be practised whenever both Kochab and Polaris are visible. I call the device Polarum because it sounds Latin and pretentious.

The nocturnal

Polarum is based on an ancient timekeeping device called a nocturnal. Prior to the invention of the chronometer, navigators in the northern hemisphere used the apparent rotation of certain stars around the Pole

Star to tell the time at night. The stars generally used were Kochab in the Little Bear or Dubhe in the Great Bear (see 'The longitude game'). In the northern night sky, these circumpolar stars appear to rotate around the Pole Star in an anti-clockwise direction about 361° every 24 hours.

The basic design of a nocturnal consisted of a circular metal or wooden plate with a hole in the centre and an extending rotating arm. Time was obtained from the nocturnal by sighting the Pole Star through the centre of the plate and lining up the selected star on the edge of the arm which rotated over a time-scale.

A nocturnal and a polarum

The star's additional daily rotation of almost 1° resulted in a 'clock' that gained a little each day. For example, early in May, Kochab appears directly above the Pole Star at midnight local time. Early in November, however, midnight occurs when Kochab is directly below the Pole Star. This problem was overcome by the addition of a second dial which adjusted the time scale according to the date of the observation. By the late 18th century, with the advent of John Harrison's chronometer, nocturnals had been discarded and few have survived.

Polarum

As explained in the last project, when Kochab lies directly above the
Pole Star, it is almost directly above the observer's longitude. As the
Earth turns towards the east, the star appears to move
in an anti-clockwise direction around the Pole Star.
Polarum is designed to measure the angle
through which the star has rotated since it
appeared directly above the Pole Star and
therefore almost directly over the observer's
longitude. Corrected for a small discrepancy,
this angle is simply the difference between the
observer's longitude and the star's 'longitude'
at the time of the observation. If the star's
longitude is known, it is a fairly easy task to
apply the angle measured by Polarum and calculate
the observer's longitude.

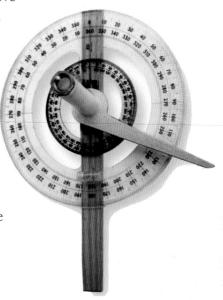

Making a simple version of Polarum

Materials

- A 360° angle measure with a rotating arm

- A larger 360° protractor with 0.5° graduations

- A short wooden arm

- A short length of 22mm plastic piping

- A spirit level bubble

- A bottle of night paint

1. Drill a small hole (the 'pole hole') through the centre of the two
   protractors.

2. Mount both on a wooden support and extend a rotating arm to
   the outer scale.

3. An 8cm length of 22mm plastic piping from a DIY store fits neatly
   over the front of the rotating pointer and provides a sighting aid
   for holding the plane of the instrument at right angles to the
   direction of the Pole Star.

4. Mount a spirit level bubble unit on the holder. Paint a thin line of fluorescent or night paint on the lower part of the level and each time you shine a torch on it the bubble will be illuminated for several minutes.

5. Another solution is to wrap the spirit level in black tape, leaving a small gap where one side of the bubble appears when the unit is level. Attach and conceal a red LED light to that end of the unit and a sharp red light will reflect from the bubble and blink through the gap when the unit is level (below). Attach the illuminated spirit level so that the gap is just visible through the 'pole hole' without obstructing the view of the Pole Star. Whichever solution is adopted, adjust the spirit level with the help of a plumb-line and check the setting at different levels of elevation.

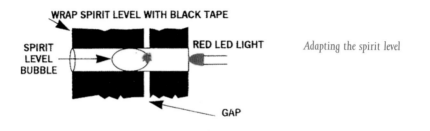

Adapting the spirit level

To use your Polarum

Close one eye and hold the device up in the night sky so that Polaris, the Pole Star, is visible through the hole. Rotate the pointer until it coincides with Kochab . Use the anti-clockwise 360° scale to find the angle of rotation. The accuracy of the device will depend on how accurately you can hold it upright and in line with the Pole Star.

The calculations

With a nautical almanac available, a Polarum reading may be used to find longitude within seconds, as the following example shows.

Stage 1. Take and time an observation of Kochab

Date and time of observation: 21h37m04s GMT on 25 January 2002
Observed angle of Kochab: 210.5°

Stage 2. Calculate the GHA of Kochab

GHA of Aries: 089.28°
Addition for Kochab: 137.55°
GHA of Kochab: 226.83°
(An observer at Greenwich would obtain this angle on Polarum).

Stage 3. Compare the two readings to obtain longitude

At Greenwich, Kochab appears at 226.83° on the Polarum, but the observer sees it at 210.5°. This difference of 16.33° from Greenwich is the observer's longitude, but is it east or west? The answer lies in a simple rhyme:

> Greenwich best, longitude west
> Greenwich least, longitude east

In the example, the Greenwich hour angle of Kochab is the larger (best) so the observer is 16.33° west of Greenwich.

A trick with Kochab

Most navigators know that the altitude of the Pole Star is a useful guide to one's latitude in the northern hemisphere. An altitude of 10° should indicate a latitude of 10° north; an altitude of 51° should indicate a latitude of 51° north and so on. The Pole Star, however, does not coincide with the celestial pole but 'circles' it at about 45'. This means that the latitude will be overestimated by 45' when the Pole Star is above the celestial pole and underestimated by the same amount when it lies below it. During the 21st century, the error will gradually decrease from 45' to 30'. Fortunately, Kochab is on the opposite side of the celestial pole to the Pole Star so its position can provide a quick estimate of the error in the altitude. When Kochab is 'on top', the Pole Star is below the celestial pole (underestimates) and when Kochab is 'down below', the Pole Star is above the celestial pole (overestimates). When Kochab lies east or west of the Pole Star, the Pole Star's altitude will roughly match the observer's latitude.

To estimate the error when Kochab is at an intermediate position

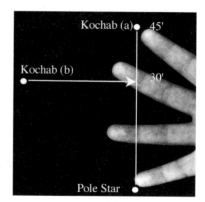

The distance from the Pole Star to Kochab is usually spanned by four outstretched fingers. Let the upright span represent the error of 45' when Kochab is above the Pole Star as at (a). With Kochab in position (b), try to estimate where it lines up on your upright scale. In the figure it is about one third down the scale, so the error of 45' has reduced by a third to 30'. If Kochab is below the Pole Star, reverse the procedure and read up the scale.

I want to be Captain

A cautionary tale for those contemplating a sailing holiday

It seemed quite a good idea at the time. We hadn't planned a summer holiday and the evenings were getting longer. Two acquaintances, Arnold and Myrtle, had invited us over for a drink and, out of the blue, they produced a video extolling the pleasures of a Mediterranean sailing holiday. The first week was to be spent in a Greek villa gradually acclimatising to the heat, the food and the drink; the second, in a flotilla of yachts, exploring idyllic islands and visiting friendly tavernas. It was, as the video explained, 'the ideal compromise between a shore-based holiday and a holiday afloat.' A holiday should never be a compromise.

Apart from the fact that Arnold was a sales executive, we knew hardly anything about him. 'So how much sailing have you done?' we enquired.

Arnold brushed this aside abruptly, 'Oh you've been sailing before and I can take a three-day course during the first week.'

'Good, good,' I enthused, 'But have you ever actually been sailing?'

'Look,' he replied, 'The brochure says the winds are only force three to four. It'll be a doddle.'

'And I'm going to learn how to swim,' added Myrtle encouragingly.

For a brief moment, I heard the Meltemi wind howling down the mountains, and saw a tangle of fouled anchors, then Arnold was waving an application form in my face. 'Shall we hire a spinnaker? It's only sixty quid extra and what's sixty quid?'

Following an explanation that this was not a high-powered skiff for nipping ashore, his enthusiasm for this optional extra waned. But we were gradually drawn into the spirit of the occasion and, in the early hours of the morning, the First Mate and I departed unsteadily to the sound of Zorba's Dance thundering in our ears.

So the weeks flew by until one afternoon in August we were bouncing along in a coach on a dusty Greek road: four adults and their two teenage daughters in search of adventure. Ahead, the deserted prison island of Makronisos shimmered in the sun, and somewhere beyond the horizon, across a sparkling turquoise sea, lay the cruising grounds. Our arrival at the sailing club was greeted by an energetic team of young Brits, Australians and New Zealanders who cheerfully escorted us to spacious and comfortable villas perched along the edge of a rocky cove. The water below looked so inviting that within minutes the two girls were diving from the rocks and beckoning us to join them. That evening, strolling down to the welcome barbecue, we helped ourselves to grapes clustering on overhanging vines and were serenaded by a thousand cicadas. There was not a single mosquito in sight.

The next morning it was all systems go. The two girls enrolled in the junior club and joined a training session on how to right a capsized dinghy. Myrtle watched them anxiously from the beach so we steered her in the direction of the local shops. Arnold strolled purposefully towards a group taking the three-day sailing course, whilst I attended the briefing for flotilla skippers. The sailing manager, a formidable lady, showed us how to use the radio and operate an engine. Later, she tested our competence at basic manoeuvres, and it was clear that she wouldn't suffer fools gladly. Indeed, one or two of us discovered that our 'many years of sailing experience' were merely one year's bad experience repeated many times. Anyway, in winds gusting around force five to six, we enjoyed an exhilarating sail and returned to the bar to receive our skippers' certificates.

Alas, the holiday of a lifetime lasted until 4.15. That was the time on the bar clock when First Mate approached looking quite crestfallen. 'Arnold's returned from his sailing course and he's in a terrible state, I think he's going to need a lot of reassurance.'

Our companion was distraught. 'You've no idea what it's like out there!' he exclaimed as I entered the villa. 'It's going to take at least four people to sail one of those things, and Myrtle can't swim so she won't be any help. She could be killed if that boom thing swings across and hits her.'

I tried to reassure him that the boats could be sailed single-handed but he wasn't having any of it.

'You think so? Do you realise that the average wind force here is six to seven? It's the Meltemi season!' All that was missing was the cello music from *Jaws*.

We thought that a strong drink might calm him down, but it only had the opposite effect.

'There's an incredible amount to this sailing business. Do you know we could have spent most of the afternoon learning all about navigation?'

I tried humouring him. 'Don't worry too much about that. I'll admit my Merchant Navy career was undistinguished, but we never got lost.' Now this was not entirely true: there was a deeply embarrassing incident in New York harbour involving a Black Star Line freighter, but this was not the moment to be candid. For the rest of the evening, Arnold insisted on describing all the potential disasters which might occur whilst sailing around the islands. Myrtle listened intently to her husband's comforting words and we noticed how her morale was starting to ebb. That night, the First Mate thought she heard a mosquito in the bedroom.

The following day, Arnold suggested that we would do well to join him on the sailing course, but his offer was declined because we had another plan. When he was safely out of the way, we took Myrtle out on one of the day yachts moored in the cove and sailed to Cape Sounion. The purpose of this expedition was to admire the ruins of a temple perched on the cliffs, but our hidden agenda was to give her back some confidence. In fact, despite some heavy seas breaking over the foredeck on the return leg, she thoroughly enjoyed the trip.

Back at the club, we relaxed until Arnold returned from his course. He was in a difficult mood and plied us with questions:

'OK then, how much anchor chain should you normally let out?' or 'OK then, what should you do when you have a man overboard situation?' or 'OK then, how do you moor when there's only one person left aboard?'

We answered him to the best of our ability, but there were two phrases which we were starting to detest. One was 'OK then', for it heralded another question drawn from the copious notes which he had scribbled during the course. The other was 'You think so?' which, more often than not, was accompanied by a contemptuous sneer. That evening, a mosquito bit my big toe (starboard).

By the end of his sailing course, Arnold appeared to have undergone a considerable change of personality. At night, he sat in the bar explaining, with great authority, the finer points of sailing and offering to take anyone who needed extra practice for a spin.

'What's a topping lift for, Arnold?'

'Oh, its er... a minor adjustment. I wouldn't worry about it if I were you.'

We listened to this mutual exchange of ignorance in disbelief, but Myrtle seemed impressed. Indeed, one good lady leaned across and announced that we were very fortunate in having an expert like Arnold accompanying us. 'Yes,' said Myrtle proudly, 'and he belongs to Mensa.'

How this transformation from nervous anxiety to supreme confidence had occurred was a complete mystery, but we now found that we had to bear the brunt of a querulous nature as well.

'Why do the children always put their elbows on the table at meals?'

It was all getting a little bit unpleasant and we couldn't understand why. Here, at the villa, there was room to escape, but what of the second week when we would be living on top of each other? Our hearts sank and we faced the rest of the holiday with considerable apprehension. That night, the mosquitoes attacked in force.

At the start of the second week, we travelled to the island of Poros by Hydrofoil to join the flotilla. These Russian-built sea monsters sped aggressively from one island to the next. We watched two collide and were determined to give them a wide berth. On the quayside, Joe, the flotilla leader from New Zealand, and Dave, his Australian engineer, showed us around our yacht *Poseidon* and outlined the various cruising procedures. Joe warned us not to waste our drinking water, but his parting shot, 'So guys, don't wash your decks in it', caused a temporary misunderstanding. Ask a New Zealander to repeat that line and you'll catch my drift. Dave explained the workings of the engine, and we complimented him on his lucid description.

'Well,' he observed, 'I've spent a lot of time on this little bastard. No worries!' It sounded ominous but we let it pass.

As we prepared for departure, Arnold took me aside. 'How are we going to play this, then?'

Initially, I was confused and assured him that he and Myrtle could have the main cabin; we would be quite happy in stern berths.

'No, you misunderstand. I've done the three-day course and I've acquired a lot of specialised knowledge which you don't have.'

It suddenly dawned on me that Arnold desperately wanted to be skipper and that this had played on his mind for several days. I assured him that I would be happy to sail under his leadership, but checked this arrangement with Joe before leaving.

Joe gave a broad grin, 'I think we'll both be keeping a close eye on him.'

Somewhat to our surprise, it all went quite well. Once in charge of operations, Arnold appeared more relaxed than he had been for several days. He attended the morning quayside briefings punctually and made detailed notes on every minute aspect of the cruise. He avoided having anything to do with the sails or the anchor, but thoroughly enjoyed taking the helm. Of course, there were the occasional collisions in tightly packed harbours, and the time when he ordered the anchor to be released in 300 fathoms. I even recall his ability to plot our position within an error of ten miles, but this is carping. Indeed, if anyone made a stupid error, it was me. I accidentally released the topping lift, just a minor adjustment – nothing to worry about, and Arnold received a very painful blow from the boom.

In the middle of the week, there was a dramatic change in the weather. An angry northerly wind, our friend the Meltemi, had returned and we became separated from the flotilla. After a fruitless search for sheltered moorings, we were forced to anchor during a rainstorm in Spetses harbour. Working from the dinghy, I laid out a second anchor and then took a stern line to a tree ashore. Anxious faces peered down, briefly illuminated by the glare of a lighthouse stabbing the darkness. 'What on earth are you doing?' exclaimed our skipper. 'I was just taking some precautions,' I replied, shaking the mud from my hands. 'There's nothing about that here,' said Arnold waving his thick wedge of notes. He remained unconvinced and ordered Myrtle to pack their cases for a night in the nearest hotel. We ferried them ashore to the beach, then, laden like sherpas, struggled to the top of some cliffs, from which could be heard the tinkle of bells. After stumbling around in the dark, they found a track leading to the town, and marched away escorted by a herd of goats. Anyway, the good news is that, later that evening, Arnold relented and returned with Myrtle to be with his crew. The bad news is that someone had sneaked alongside and pinched the dinghy.

Despite the Meltemi, the holiday was drawing to a satisfactory conclusion. Joe and his splendid team were always close at hand to solve any real problems, and we had enjoyed several lively evenings ashore with the other crews. But fate has a nasty habit of striking when it is least expected, and it was lurking in the narrow stretch of water between Skilli Island and the mainland. The flotilla was returning to Poros and Joe had advised us to use this gap as a short cut but to have our engines ready as the seas there were unpredictable. Arnold decided to make the journey entirely by engine, but reluctantly agreed to our raising the mainsail. The girls soon became bored and went below to play cards.

After lurching along in lumpy seas for a couple of hours, *Poseidon* reached the gap, only to be confronted by *Georgio*, an inter-island battering ram heading in our direction. Fortunately, it failed to score, but while we were being tossed around in its wake our engine started to cough.

'What are you doing?' screamed Arnold.

'Nothing,' I replied, 'But I think we have a problem – you better get your notes out.'

The engine spluttered and died, and the yacht started to wallow alarmingly. Arnold leaped down into the cabin, or rather the cabin reared up to meet him, and having regained his footing, he pressed the starting motor several times. The engine refused to budge.

'Right,' he cried, 'Everyone get below!' and Myrtle fled the cockpit leaving us to contemplate heavy seas breaking on the jagged rocks of an approaching reef.

Keeping the bows up to wind, we set the headsail and off went *Poseidon* like an ocean greyhound. Having cleared the reef and set a course for Poros, we paused for a breather and looked down into the saloon. Arnold was pounding the VHF radio in desperation, 'Mayday! Mayday!', and Myrtle had fainted. The two girls were still playing cards.

A rather subdued *Poseidon* approached Poros that afternoon. The support boat met us at the harbour entrance and our friend Dave removed an airlock from the fuel pipe. No worries. Arnold sat alone in silence on the foredeck. Despite assurances that we had never been in serious danger, Myrtle wept hysterically. 'Weren't you terrified back there?' she cried, 'We could have lost our lives!'

One of us muttered, 'Better than losing those ***** notes,' and then we concentrated on making a final approach to the berth.

At that moment, Arnold stepped into the cockpit and, pushing us aside, resumed command. Sensing a familiar hand on her tiller, *Poseidon* ploughed with a sickening crunch into the concrete walls of the quayside.

That evening, the flotilla held a final get-together in a lively taverna. After the meal, Joe made a short speech and awarded a prize to one member of each crew. He gave a tin of spinach to a diminutive lady who was always seen tugging at her anchor, and a pair of water-wings to the airline pilot who fell overboard in Hydra. There was a toy telephone for the Birmingham businessman who insisted on a daily fax from his office, and a tourist map for the family that accidentally sailed halfway to Crete. The skipper of *Poseidon* received a rather smart little sailing hat with a Greek inscription. Before leaving the taverna, we asked one of the waiters for a translation. It read, 'I want to be captain.' According to our shipmates, the mosquitoes were very busy that night, but we slept soundly.

Steering by the stars

Steering towards a star is less tiring than staring at a compass, but the stars gradually change their direction and height as they move across the sky. For years, I searched for a simple rule of thumb to estimate how much a star's bearing would alter in an hour. The first

book I ever consulted on this topic, a dog-eared 1930s guide for navigators, was most eloquent in its description of the heavens, but offered not a single clue. 'Lo! With a beckoning urge, Orion climbs majestically from the horizon to mark the slow path of your argosy' – that sort of thing. A more recent publication suggests that as long as the star does not rise too high in the heavens, 15° an hour should suffice. To this one might add 'give or take 10°.'

Well here is a solution which, unless you voyage in very high latitudes, should be reasonably accurate and can be used in conjunction with the hand-measured angles as described on page 32.

East/west stars

By using stars that lie to the east or west, there is a quick way of estimating how much their bearings will change in one hour and it's good for any latitude between 0° and 45°. Simply divide your latitude by 4. So in latitude 36° the change is about 9° per hour. Above latitude 45°, this formula gradually overestimates the change of bearing and a more accurate result will be obtained if you divide your latitude by 5. In the northern hemisphere these stars move to your right and in the southern hemisphere they move to your left.

Stars in the direction of the poles

In this direction, the stars 'rotate' around their celestial poles and their hourly bearings can vary considerably. Nevertheless, the rule above can be used – but only with stars that are very low on the horizon, and these are often difficult to see.

Stars in the direction of the equator

As you look towards the equator, the rate of change increases with the star's height. To work out the hourly change, estimate the star's altitude and add it to your latitude; then, as before, divide by 4 or 5.

Example (a)

In latitude 16°, stars to the east or west will progress at roughly $16°/4 = 4°$ per hour. Horizon stars in the direction of the nearest pole will progress at about the same rate. A star in the direction of the equator with an altitude of 20° will progress at approximately $(16° + 20°)/4 = 9°$ per hour. A star with an altitude of 40° will progress at approximately $(16° + 40°)/4 = 14°$ per hour.

Example (b)

In latitude 55°, stars to the east or west will progress at approximately $55°/5 = 11°$ per hour. Horizon stars in the direction of the nearest pole will progress at about the same rate. A star in the direction of the equator with an altitude of 20° will progress at approximately $(55° + 20°)/5 = 15°$ per hour. A star with an altitude of 40° will progress at approximately $(55° + 40°)/5 = 19°$ per hour.

Follow that star

To follow a course using a star that is dead ahead and moving 12° an hour to the right, gradually adjust its relative bearing over an hour until it is 12° to starboard. An easier solution is to keep steering half the angle (in this case 6° or three fingers at arm's length) to its left and after an hour you'll end up right on course. In either case, if the star doesn't coincide with your intended course, align it with something on the boat and apply the same procedure. Whichever you choose, it would be wise to check the compass at regular intervals in case you inadvertently follow a different star and end up retracing the slow path of your argosy.

Plumb-line navigation

Plumb-line navigation is an old method of finding a course or a bearing when two stars appear in a vertical line. For example, when the Southern Cross constellation appears upright, the upper and lower stars point almost directly south. Similarly, when the sides of the square of Pegasus appear upright they point almost directly north (or south).

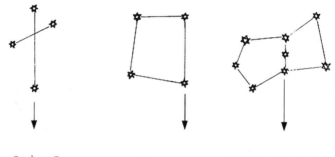

Southern Cross   Pegasus   Orion (southern hemisphere)

The Pacific Islanders had an amazing repertoire of navigational techniques. Their use of zenith or overhead stars as a guide to latitude, and of horizon stars as a compass, is well documented and they seem to have used plumb-line navigation too. For example, seafarers in the Tokelau group are known to have navigated with the help of Orion's belt. When the three stars of the belt were perpendicular to the horizon, it indicated the course to steer between two main islands.

    These early voyagers had no knowledge of latitude or longitude, nor had they chronometers or charts as we know them, but they had the stars and their masts to line them up. Observing the night sky from an island, they would have seen that the movement of the heavens caused certain pairs of stars to line up vertically in the same place each night. That this vertical alignment occurred briefly, and a little earlier the following night, was of no great significance. What mattered was that the stars rotated to form a reliable signpost in the sky. During a voyage, if a signpost was observed ahead or astern of a sailing craft, the same stars could be used as a guide for the return voyage.

On long voyages, as the height of the signpost above the horizon increased or decreased, its movement would provide a celestial record of the distance covered. For example, by keeping the nightly signpost formed by Sirius and Procyon dead ahead, a craft sailing from the east coast of New Zealand will eventually sight the island of Raratonga. At the start of the voyage, Procyon, the lower of the pair, would be about 30° above the horizon (one outstretched hand and one fist) Approaching Raratonga, it would have risen to about 60° above the horizon (three outstretched hands).

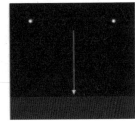

The signpost need not necessarily be vertical. For example, in the Marquesas Islands, Canopus rises in the south-east and is followed by Sirius in the east. Within a couple of hours, these two bright stars are parallel with the horizon and by steering between them when they attain this position each night, a craft will eventually reach Easter Island 1,800 miles away.

This type of navigation is not without its shortcomings. A signpost is only visible for a short period each night, and may only be visible in the night sky for a few months. Furthermore, it is essential to maintain the initial track to ensure a reliable return path; ocean currents, weather, leeway and changes of tack may divert a craft from its route. Here are two examples of how this technique may be used. The first will be of interest to ocean navigators, and the second to those whose voyages are of a local or less adventurous nature.

Ocean navigating

When two stars appear in a vertical line the arrangement can be seen by anyone situated along a particular line across the earth's surface. The path of this track or 'great circle' is found by joining a line between the two points on the earth lying directly below the stars and extending it across the globe.

To find your position line you need a way of determining when one star is directly above the other. You also require a method of plotting the track or great circle along which you are situated. Though it has its limitations at sea, a short plumb-line can be used, but it will require some steadying by hand. The plumb bob could be immersed

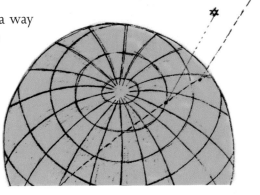

in liquid to reduce oscillations. Another method is to use a spirit level which has a bubble unit set at right angles to the straight edge – these are readily available at hardware stores. A thin line of luminous or night paint below the bubble unit will help it to glow in the dark. A mirror may also be used – attach the bubble unit to one end of the small mirror and, with the bubble in front of your eye, manoeuvre the mirror until the reflection of the upper star appears to coincide with the lower star and the bubble is level.

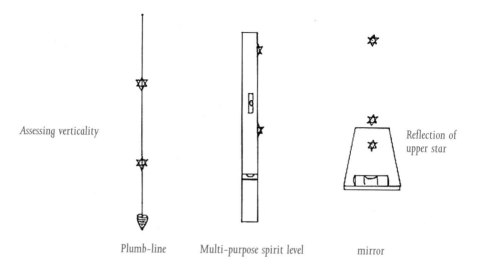

Assessing verticality

Reflection of upper star

Plumb-line   *Multi-purpose spirit level*   mirror

A gnomonic chart is essential for plotting the position line. In the gnomonic projection, the shortest distance between two points on the surface of the earth is shown as a straight line. Several of these charts are available to help navigators plot great circle routes across the major oceans of the world. Admiralty chart no. 5098 is ideal for this procedure, and although it covers the South Pacific and Southern Oceans, it may be reversed for use in the Northern Hemisphere. The meridians printed on the chart may be renumbered to meet the needs of the situation, and a covering of adhesive transparent film will prevent wear and tear.

Armed with the date and GMT of the observation, the declinations and Greenwich hour angles of the two stars can be obtained from an almanac. These are the equivalent of the stars' earthly latitude and longitude and are plotted directly on the gnomonic chart. A straight line drawn from the lower star's position, and continued through the highest star's position, will eventually pass through the observer's position. Here is an example of the technique using two stars in the Great Bear, which were observed in a vertical line from the position to the South of the Madeira:

Date: 12 March 2003. **Time:** 22h38m20s GMT

Stars	GHA	Declination
Upper (Phecda)	331.3° (i.e. 28.7° east)	53.7° north
Lower (Mizar)	308.8° (i.e. 51.2° east)	54.9° north

Gnomonic plot

A line extended from the two stars ...

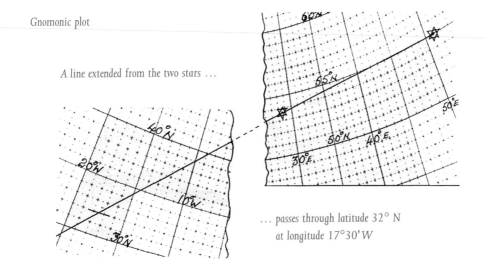

... passes through latitude 32° N at longitude 17°30'W

The illustration presents the observation plotted on a gnomonic chart. One section contains the positions of the stars at the time of the observation, and the other shows an extension of the line drawn from them. In latitude 32° north, for example, the line passes through longitude 17°30' west. If neither latitude nor longitude is known then further lines can be obtained from other pairs of stars and plotted to fix the vessel's position. Star pairs that lie close to the celestial poles are beyond the scope of the gnomonic chart mentioned above. For these situations, a polar gnomonic projection is required.

Local navigation

If your sailing is confined to a specific area, you can compile a collection of vertical star pairs and the bearings associated with them. The results may be used to check the compass or to provide 'signposts' which may guide you to the entrance of a river or an anchorage, or to avoid an obstruction or a shallow bank. For example, the signpost formed by Procyon and Sirius that points to Raratonga from New Zealand can, in spring, lead you out of the Solent. It can also guide you from Brighton Marina and straight on to the Casquet Rocks near Alderney.

If there are no suitable star pairs, a single bright star may be used to provide a reliable compass bearing. When the star is on a particular bearing, its height above the horizon is checked and noted for future use. For example, in latitude 50° north when Aldebaran, which lies close to the constellation of Orion, is bearing due east or west, it is about 22° above the horizon. That's roughly the width of a well-stretched hand at arm's length.

All this suggests that a thorough knowledge of the stars is required. On the contrary, you don't even need to know their names, but you must have a reliable way of identifying them from the celestial backdrop. Also, make sure that they twinkle and are not wandering planets. Sailing on summer nights, I am often guided from the sea to the entrance of a creek by a Y-shaped group of stars setting to the west. They are not all members of the same constellation, but if the sky is clear they are always there. It would be easy to check the compass or switch on the GPS but the satisfaction that comes from using the stars to guide me home is immeasurable.

Appendix 1. Tide abacus scales

TIME SCALE

4.0h	4.5h	5.0h	5.5h	6.0h	6.5h	7.0h
						.45
						.30
					.15	.15
					6.0h	6.0h
				.45	.45	.45
				.30	.30	.30
			.15	.15	.15	.15
			5.0h	5.0h	5.0h	5.0h
		.45	.45	.45	.45	.45
		.30	.30	.30	.30	.30
	.15	.15	.15	.15	.15	.15
	4.0h	4.0h	4.0h	4.0h	4.0h	4.0h
.45	.45	.45	.45	.45	.45	.45
.30	.30	.30	.30	.30	.30	.30
.15	.15	.15	.15	.15	.15	.15
3.0h	3.0h	3.0h	3.0h	3.0h	3.0h	3.0h
.45	.45	.45	.45	.45	.45	.45
.30	.30	.30	.30	.30	.30	.30
.15	.15	.15	.15	.15	.15	.15
2.0h	2.0h	2.0h	2.0h	2.0h	2.0h	2.0h
.45	.45	.45	.45	.45	.45	.45
.30	.30	.30	.30	.30	.30	.30
.15	.15	.15	.15	.15	.15	.15
1.0h	1.0h	1.0h	1.0h	1.0h	1.0h	1.0h
.45	.45	.45	.45	.45	.45	.45
.30	.30	.30	.30	.30	.30	.30
.15	.15	.15	.15	.15	.15	.15

HEIGHT SCALE

4 m	4.5 m	5 m	5.5 m	6 m	6.5 m	7 m
						.75
						.50
					.25	.25
					6 m	6 m
				.75	.75	.75
				.50	.50	.50
			.25	.25	.25	.25
			5 m	5 m	5 m	5 m
		.75	.75	.75	.75	.75
		.50	.50	.50	.50	.50
	.25	.25	.25	.25	.25	.25
	4 m	4 m	4 m	4 m	4 m	4 m
.75	.75	.75	.75	.75	.75	.75
.50	.50	.50	.50	.50	.50	.50
.25	.25	.25	.25	.25	.25	.25
3 m	3 m	3 m	3 m	3 m	3 m	3 m
.75	.75	.75	.75	.75	.75	.75
.50	.50	.50	.50	.50	.50	.50
.25	.25	.25	.25	.25	.25	.25
2 m	2 m	2 m	2 m	2 m	2 m	2 m
.75	.75	.75	.75	.75	.75	.75
.50	.50	.50	.50	.50	.50	.50
.25	.25	.25	.25	.25	.25	.25
1 m	1 m	1 m	1 m	1 m	1 m	1 m
.75	.75	.75	.75	.75	.75	.75
.50	.50	.50	.50	.50	.50	.50
.25	.25	.25	.25	.25	.25	.25

Appendix 2. Almanac data for use with sundial

January

1	23 S	1204
5		1205
7		1206
9		1207
10	22	1208
16	21	1210
21	20	1211
25	19	1212
29	18	1213

February

2	17	1214
5	16	
8	15	
11	14	
14	13	
17	12	
20	11	1214
23	10	1213
25	9	
28	8	

March

3	7	1212
5	6	1212
8	5	1211
10	4	1210
13	3	
15	2	1209
18	1	1208
21	0	1207
23	1 N	
26	2	1206
28	3	1205
31	4	1204

April

3	5	1203
5	6	
8	7	1202
11	8	1201
13	9	
16	10	1200
19	11	1159
22	12	
25	13	1158
28	14	1157

May

1	15	1157
4	16	
8	17	1156
12	18	
16	19	
21	20	
26	21	1157

June

1	22	1158
10	23	1159
14		1200
19	23.5	1201
24	23.5	1202
28		1203

July

3	23	1204
12	22	1205
18	21	1206
23	20	
28	19	

August

1	18	
5	17	1206
9	16	1205
12	15	
15	14	1204
19	13	
22	12	1203
25	11	1202
28	10	1201
30	9	

September

2	8	1200
5	7	1159
8	6	1158
10	5	1157
13	4	1156
16	3	1155
18	2	1154
21	1	1153
23	0	1152
26	1 S	1151
28	2	1150

October

1	3	1150
4	4	1149
6	5	1148
9	6	1147
11	7	1147
14	8	1146
17	9	1145
19	10	
22	11	
25	12	1144
28	13	
31	14	

November

3	15	
6	16	
10	17	
14	18	1144
17	19	1145
22	20	1146
28	21	1148

December

3	22	1150
6		1151
8		1152
11	23	1153
13		1154
15		1155
17		1156
19		1157
21	23.5	1158
23		1159
25		1200
27		1201
29		1202
31		1203

Appendix 3.
Vernier scales

Backstaff

Octant

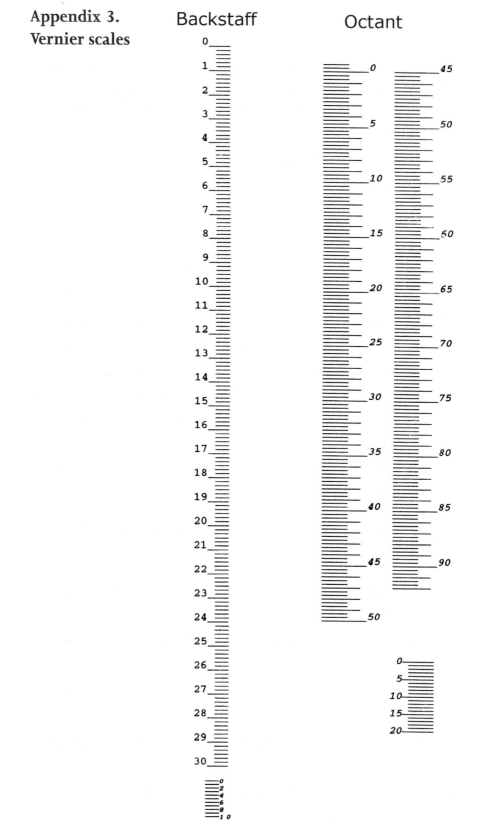

Appendix 4. GHA Aries without an almanac

If no almanac is available, the following may be used as a rough guide to finding the GHA of Aries. In a four-year cycle, Aries transits the Greenwich meridian on 21 September, at approximately the following times (GMT).

23 55 in a leap year e.g., 2004

23 56 the next year e.g., 2005

23 57 the next year e.g., 2006

23 58 the next year e.g., 2007

1. Select the appropriate time for the most recent 21 September.

2. To find the time of transit on the day of the observation, subtract 4 minutes and add 4 seconds for each day since 21 September.

3. For each hour between the transit at Greenwich and the time of the observation, multiply by 15.05°. For each minute, add 0.25° .

4. The result is the GHA of Aries if the observation is after the Greenwich transit.

    If observation is before the Greenwich transit, deduct the result from 360°.

Example. To find the GHA of Aries at 2358hrs on 6 October 2004 (leap year)

1. Greenwich transit of Aries on 21 September 2004 = 2355hrs (approx).

2. 15 days later (−60 minutes and +60 seconds) = −59 minutes difference.

3. Therefore, the Greenwich transit of Aries on 6 October 2004 = 2256hrs.

4. The observation was at 2358 = 1 hour 2 minutes after Greenwich transit.

5. 1 hour × 15.05° + 2 minutes × 0.25° = 15.55°.

6. The observation occurred after the time of the Greenwich transit so the GHA of Aries $= 15.55°$ (This result is only $0.1°$ in error).

To find the GHA of any star, add the stars SHA to the GHA of Aries. A list of stars' SHAs and their declinations will be found in any nautical almanac or an annual reference book such as *Whitaker's Almanac*.

Answers

Test your knowledge the wind (page 19)

True: 1, 2, 5, 7, 10

False: 3, 4 (only true in northern hemisphere), 6, 8, 9 (30 knots is
         force 7, a near gale)

A fatal flaw (page 30)

Had the radio operator met his unfortunate end in this way, the
contents of his dream would have remained unknown.

Rope trick (page 35)

1(b) means both lines can be released with little difficulty. By Sodde's
Law, however, a third line will have been thrown over the other two by
the time you get back from the pub.

2(a) is less likely to jam when letting go.

3(a) produces more friction to take the strain.

4(b) is less likely to jam when letting go.

Threefold puzzle (page 61)

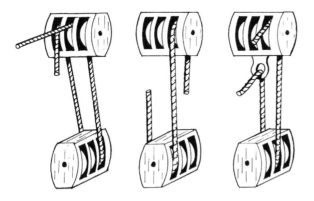

The secret lies in the way the blocks are placed one above the other.
The sheaves in one block are placed at right angles to the sheaves of
the other. As the rope leaves the top block, it leads directly to the
correct sheave in the lower block. From the lower blocks it leads up to
the correct sheave in the upper block and so on.

Survive! (page 101)

Adrift in a small boat, people often survive for several days without food or water but suffer because they have no means of attracting the attention of any passing ships. So the matches, the rope soaked in paraffin and the mirror will be of vital importance. These are followed by water and food. The sail is useful for collecting rain. The knife, fishing kit and shark repellent will also come in handy. The oar may help with signalling, catching turtles or keeping sharks at bay. The chart and the radio receiver are of little use. There are no mosquitoes and you are going nowhere special, so you needn't worry about the compass. Here is the order according to sea survival experts:

Mosquito net 14	Sail 7	Water 5
Shark repellent 11	Length of rope 3	Survival rations 6
Spare oar 8	Portable radio 13	Knife 9
Paraffin 2	Compass 15	Compact mirror 4
Pacific Ocean chart 12	Matches 1	Fishing kit 10

Did your chances of survival improve by pooling your ideas?

Bibliography

Books

Burch, David. 1986. *Emergency Navigation*. Camden, Maine:
International Marine.
A comprehensive and authoritative presentation of the principles
of navigation and pathfinding techniques.

Fisher, David. 1995. *Latitude Hooks and Azimuth Rings*. Camden, Maine:
International Marine.
How to build and use 18 traditional navigational tools.

Lewis, David. 1975. *We, the Navigators*. Honolulu:
University of Hawaii Press.
Traditional Polynesian pathfinding techniques.

Sobel, Dava. 1996. *Longitude*. London: Fourth Estate.
An interesting account of the search for ways of determining
longitude and the development of the chronometer.

Thomas, Steve. 1987. *The Last Navigator*. Camden, Maine:
International Marine.
The art of sailing-canoe navigation in Micronesia.

Some useful websites

Polynesian Voyaging Society
www.pvs-hawaii.com

Navigation techniques
www.eso.org/seaspace/navigation/navastro

History of navigation
www.nmm.ac.uk

ABOUT THE AUTHOR

Tony Crowley was born in Richmond,
Yorkshire in 1940. As a boy, living by the Suez Canal,
he learnt to sail using a converted wartime seaplane float.
The Duke of York's Royal Military School convinced him that
the sea was a more suitable career and he worked for several years
as a deck officer in the merchant ships of various countries. He has
worked as an entertainer, playing a one-man-band on TV programmes
such as *Rainbow, Jim'll Fix It, How* and *What's my line?*. He has written
many careers books for schools and has contributed articles on
emergency navigation and short stories to *Navigation News,
Ocean Navigator, Practical Boat Owner, The Nautical Magazine*
and *The Seafarer*. Married to a saint (Teresa) with
four children and five grandchildren, he sails
for pleasure on a battered Westerly 22,
plays the banjo and supports
Sheffield Wednesday FC.

✴